MALTA during the First World War

ANTHONY ZARB-DIMECH

1914-1918

First edition cover

Cover images
Front, top: A St John Ambulance Association Malta Centre colour postcard which was sold to raise funds for the wounded in Gallipoli.
Bottom: A view of man tents and P.O.W.'s facing Fort Verdala, Cottonera.

Back, top: Turkish P.O.W.'s at Verdala barracks, Cottonera.
Bottom: The access way into St Clement's prison camp, Cottonera.
(Images courtesy of Mr John A. Mizzi)

First edition, 2004
This edition, 2014

Copyright © Anthony Zarb-Dimech – anthonyzd7@gmail.com

Distributed by BDL Books. 13, Giorgio Preca Street, San Ġwann SGN3511
info@bdlbooks.com – 21380351 – www.bdlbooks.com

ISBN: 978-99932-0-306-3

DEDICATED TO THE
FALLEN MALTESE AND GOZITANS
OF THE GREAT WAR

On the occasion of the centenary commemoration of the commencement of the First World War, I have been solicited to reprint the first issue of *Malta during the First World War 1914–1918* that I had published a decade ago and which, to my surprise, was all sold out. Whilst feeling grateful for this positive response that I had received, I am taking the cudgel once more through Book Distributors Ltd (BDL) to have it reprinted. As all historians and lovers of history are cognizant of the fact that historical research is always 'on the move' in the sense that the more one involves himself/herself in such an undertaking, the more he or she is liable to elicit further 'discoveries' and even perhaps corrections here and there. So, although I did my best to be as documentative as possible and as I have been hard-pressed in time to expedite this second edition, it may be that some detail here and there may have escaped my attention or lacking, perhaps, some elucidation and, whilst begging pardon for such an infringement, if any, I would be quite pleased with any reader who may point out such a shortcoming, I repeat, if any.

Anthony Zarb-Dimech
June, 2014

CONTENTS

4.8	Wyndlham Levy Grech (1890–1956) and other Maltese RAF personnel	54
4.9	Zeppelin Raid!	56
5	**Malta Dockyard and Grand Harbour**	**58**
5.1	The importance of the Dockyard	58
5.2	The workforce	60
5.3	Ordnance Stores (*Polverista*)	61
5.4	Explosion at Ordnance Stores	62
5.5	French Navy	65
5.6	HMS *Melita*	65
5.7	The Emergence of Trade Unionism	66
6	**HMS *Louvain***	**67**
6.1	World War One (Naval War)	67
6.2	Feeder Lines	68
6.3	World War One U-boats	71
6.4	The Sinking of HMS *Louvain*	74
6.5	UC 22	80
7	**Hospital Facilities**	**82**
7.1	Casualties of the Great War	82
7.2	Transport of casualties	85
7.3	Hospital Ships	86
7.4	The Red Cross and St John's Ambulance Work	88
7.5	Hospitals	93
7.6	Tas-Sliema and First World War Casualties	101
8	**The Gozitan Casualties**	**108**
8.1	Gozitan Casualties	110
9	**Prisoners of War**	**113**
9.1	Standing Orders	113
9.2	The captain crew of the German cruiser *'Emdem'*	116
9.3	Karl Doenitz	117

Foreword

On the 28 June 2014 the world marks the 100th Anniversary of the commencement of the First World War. The deadly magnitude of the Great War (1914–1918) had passed into the pages of history as a ray of hope to end all wars. This was not to be as another much greater and devastating world conflict was to afflict this planet between the years 1939–1945.

In *Malta during the First World War 1914–1918,* the author covers the main areas of direct relevance to Malta during the Great War. He introduces the reader by placing him in context in his exposition about the background to the years preceding the war. He proceeds with war mobilisation in Malta soon after the proclamation of hostilities. The logical sequence of the topics continues with the role of the then, HM Dockyard, the Gallipoli campaign, the role of the King's Own Malta Regiment of Militia and the Royal Malta Artillery, Aviation, The Malta Dockyard and Grand Harbour, HMS *Louvain,* Hospital facilities, Gozitan casualties, Prisoners of War, War Graves and Memorials, Social Administration and the role played by women. He aptly concludes with an overview of the aftermath and the military heritage bequeathed from the British era.

The flow of information is very helpful and the book is a very good reference map for the reader to delve deeper in the areas of interest under study. The book may be easily considered not only as an intense historical research but a simple and understandable guide to an important period of Maltese history. Although many books have been written about Malta's legendary Second World War role, relatively less is known about Malta's contribution during the First World War.

The text is well supplemented with Appendices giving statistics of Maltese officers and men who served in Malta and overseas, the

Register of names of the Maltese and Gozitan seamen who died between the years 1918–1921, list of Gozitan servicemen who sacrificed their lives during the war and First World War relief funds. Other documents and photos have added no small amount of emotion and mingle well with the rest of the material.

The author's direct interest in the subject is evident throughout the text particularly in the chapter dedicated to HMS *Louvain*. As the author rightly ponders, all wars leave a scar of sorrow and comparisons between wars are indeed odious.

This book is a splendid follow-up to the author's last publication titled, *'Moments in Time – An Album of an Old Maltese Family'*. This pattern has already been put forward by the author in his other publications, titled, *'Taking Cover – A History of Air-Raid Shelters: Malta 1940–1943* followed by *'Mobilisation in Action – A History of Civil Defence: Malta 1940–1943'*.

On a personal note, I was more than glad to assist my friend Anthony in his research not only because I also suffered a family loss when my great-grandfather Mr Carmelo Xuereb (who was a 2nd class Officers' Cook on HMS *Louvain*) died when HMS *Louvain* was torpedoed, but also because of my great interest in the subject.

Andrew Cauchi
2004

PREFACE

Malta's small size and strategic location at the crossroads of the Mediterranean and on the farthest European periphery have always drawn the attention of many an Empire, which sought to exploit the Islands natural endowments (mainly natural harbour facilities and manpower) as a launching pad to expand further their control over vast areas of the world. The Crimean War of 1854–56 (this year marks the 150th Anniversary of its commencement) established Malta as a Naval base for the British Empire, which until then was still undecided as to whether to use Malta, Cyprus or Corfù.

Since time immemorial, Malta's role had been subservient until it achieved independence and freed from its military base role in 1964 and 1979 respectively. The First and Second World Wars are a classical example of the manifestation of this servility.

During the Second World War (1940–1943) some 7,000 Maltese and foreign (civilians and servicemen) lost their lives in the defence of Malta, both on land, sea and air, both in Malta and overseas. In the First World War, although Malta was not directly attacked, nearly 600 Maltese servicemen died in war action whilst serving overseas.

Malta's legendary role in the Second World War, in what is described as the second Great Siege of Malta (after that of 1565) has, to an extent overshadowed, but not diminished the important part Malta played during the Great War (1914–1918).

Comparisons are indeed odious and the scope of the material is not to contrast the tragic loss of relatives, poverty and suffering brought on the Maltese population in both wars, or on the significance of each war episodes. Both must be seen and appreciated in their own separate wider historical events.

Malta during the First World War 1914–1918 explores in reference book format those aspects of the First World War, that are of direct relevance to Malta that merit closer and more detailed attention. This book focuses, amongst others, on Education, Health, Aviation, Memorials and Cemeteries, Hospitals and Nursing and personal experiences. The book seeks to form a comprehensive and concise presentation of this period of Maltese history.

The book is based on references from numerous texts both English and Maltese as well as archived reports and other documentation and the stories of next-of-kin as recounted to them by their relatives who lived the war years. Photos and official documents have also been consulted and where possible presented.

I felt the need to go into this research, not only as a dedication and tribute to my grandmother's brother, Assistant Engineer John Ellul who lost his life in the sinking of HMS *Louvain* in January 1918, (70 Maltese crew and ratings died in this tragedy), and also to the other Maltese servicemen who lost their lives during the Great War, but also because our history is rich and deserves more codification and organisation, as new material is unearthed. In this way more value is added on to our Heritage and Culture.

CHAPTER 1

MALTA AND THE GREAT WAR

(1914–1918)

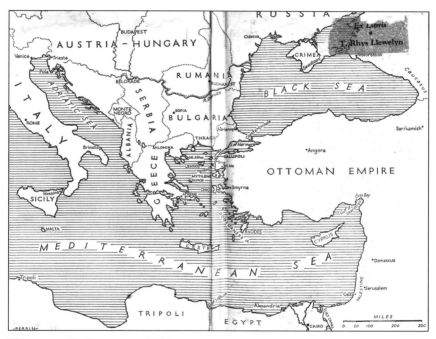

The eastern Mediterranean 1914

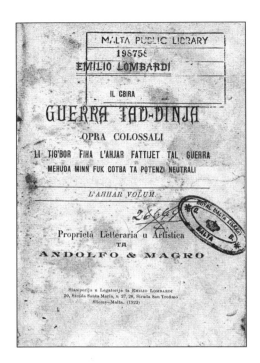

Possibly the first ever comprehensive history in the Maltese language of the Great War printed at Emilio Lombardi press dated 1922 (in four volumes) by Andolfo & Magro. Shortly after the termination of hostilities, the Malta Historical Society appointed a board to write an account of what happened in our Islands during the eventful quadrienium, 1914–1918

1.1   Wars

Throughout history men fought for great principles; social equality, democratic government and nationalism. Since Plato and Aristotle and other great philosophers such as John Locke, Tom Pain, Voltaire and Rousseau, wars have been fought with such regular frequency leaving millions killed in senseless and bloody actions. Revolutions (such as the French and Russian revolutions) and wars in many countries were caused by people who felt strongly about ideals: privileges or rights they wanted.

Wars are also a source of revenue to the armaments industry and while the owners of such firms sit pretty on piles of cash and other income generated by this business, they put pressure on politicians both in an orthodox and unorthodox fashion to 'create' wars in the name of some ideal.

1.2   Main Trends and Events 1914

During the 20th Century, the world experienced a second phase of revolution, this time in industry. Division of labour and specialisation of tasks in manufacturing led to mass production. Men like Henry Ford in America paved the way to mechanisation in industry. Industrialism brought about changes caused by these new methods of production and new inventions. The growth of factories caused the growth of towns and created the possibility for the poor classes of society to buy what had formerly been available for the wealthy.

Gradually, all the countries of Western Europe became industrialised and this led to great competition for world markets. Britain faced stiff competition. A new sea route to the east was created by the **cutting of the Suez Canal in 1869**, in which both France and Britain were interested. It led them to take control of the government of Egypt, though only Britain took part in crushing the revolt against this foreign control that occurred in 1882, resulting in stronger British influence in Egypt.

Most of the world in 1914 had been divided among the Great Powers, and this period could be described as one of international rivalry between Britain, France, Germany, Belgium, Italy and Portugal. This rivalry, which was reaching unprecedented heights, was leading to inevitable war and these Powers started to arrange into spheres of influence or groups. Britain became friendly with France, and as time went by with Russia, whilst Germany formed alliances with Austria and Italy. All the Powers were busy building up their military and naval forces to prepare for a war looming on the horizon. It was a situation awaiting the least spark to start off a wildfire.

THE KING'S SHIPS. REVIEWED BY HIS MAJESTY 1914.

The King's ships reviewed by his Majesty at South Sea 1914.
Sea power is a great 'enabler' and this was definitely the case in the First Word War. Britain went to war in August 1914 and having won the naval race with Germany, the British Empire controlled the seas for the duration of the conflict
(Card by courtesy of Ms Christine Scicluna)

1.3 The Start of the First World War

The First World War had been described as the most murderous of wars in the history of mankind and it all commenced when on 28 June 1914, the Archduke Franz Ferdinand and his wife, heirs to the throne of Austro-Hungary were assassinated in Sarajevo. The government in Vienna interpreted this act as a Serbian plot and after securing the support of its German ally, it submitted an ultimatum to Serbia insisting that officials from Austria be allowed to investigate the assassination. The Serbian authorities were not satisfied and evaded the Austrian request. Austria declared war on the 28 July 1914. This led to a start of the First World War. France and Germany immediately joined in. Great Britain hesitated until Germany invaded neutral Belgium, and then, came in on the side of France and Russia.

On land the 'Central Powers'(Germany, Austria-Hungary and Turkey) more than held their own, but eventually the blockage by the British Navy had its effect, in spite of the growth of submarine warfare, and in 1917 the entry into the war of the United States made up for the loss of Russia (then in the middle of internal revolution), so that in 1918 Germany and her allies were forced to accept an armistice.

The Peace Treaties that followed the war divided Europe into a number of small states, deprived Germany and her allies of their colonies, was set up the League of Nations in the hope of preventing future wars

H.G Wells described the First World War as *the war to end all wars*. But his hope proved to be an illusion as history repeated itself. The Versailles Treaty left the defeated nations like Germany vying on other nations to be vindicated. Allied nations in their turn, such as Italy felt that they did not have a good run for their money. The rise of Fascism and Nazism together with the development of Communism and Imperialism brought about an uneasy existence in Europe that only lasted for merely 20 years. A more terrible holocaust was born to spread over the corners of the world.

1.4   World War One and Two

The figures of dead resulting from the First World War are the most horrific in the history of war. Speaking in the House of Commons on 20 August 1940, the British Prime Minister, Winston Churchill drew up comparisons between the war casualties suffered up to 1940 during the Second World War. He contrasted them with those of the Great War. The result of his conclusions was based on the different strategies of war and also on the new mechanised warfare, especially aerial attacks that targeted the civilian population. The First World War was fought on battlefields such as those at

Somme and Passchendaele (that saw mass slaughters) cut off from the population; and the fronts consisted of troops attacking each other's entrenched positions and by shelling them. The fronts of the Second World War ran through the factories, roads and towns and the maintenance of a high civilian morale was equally important.

> **"...It is also useful to compare the first year of this second war against German aggression with its forerunner a quarter of a century ago. Although this war is in fact only a continuation of the last, very great differences in its character are apparent. ...The British casualties in the first 12 months of the Great War amounted to 365,000. In this war, I am thankful to say, British killed, wounded, prisons and missing, including civilians, do not exceed 92,000, and of these a large proportion are alive as prisoners of war. Looking more widely around, one may say that throughout all Europe for one man killed or wounded in the first year perhaps five were killed or wounded in 1914–1915..."[1]**

The Second World War lasted longer than the first, and was conducted with unparalleled ferocity over a larger proportion of the world's surface. The weapons used were of a greater destructive power. But, because of the horrors of the fighting in Flanders between 1914 and 1918, this is not always realised. Although the world as a whole suffered greater loss in the Second World War, Europe, especially Britain suffered more in the first. The First World War was fought in great part in Belgium and northern France, and in the swathe of misery and massacre, which stretched from Switzerland to the Belgian coast; an average of 2,000 British, French and German soldiers died every day.[2]

---

1   *The Penguin Hansard, Volume III, Britain Gathers Strength*, Taken *verbatim* from the House of Commons Official Report of Parliamentary Debates, Penguin Books, August 1941.

2   See *Purnell's History of the Second World War*, pp. 2592–2599

Keeping in mind that statistics are the third of three types of lies, and the fact that there are no reliable figures for civilian deaths for the First World War, the cost of the Second World War was far greater.

1.5   Malta at War

Sir Charles Lucas, author of the Royal Colonial Institute's history of the epic resistance of the British Empire in the great struggle under the title *The Empire at War* had this to say when speaking at a lecture delivered at the Royal Colonial Institute by Dr Augusto Bartolo on 28 September 1920:

> **"I want the people of Malta to realise that it is a mistake to believe that people in England know nothing about their famous island and care less. To me, the Empire without Malta and Malta outside the Empire is inconceivable. They are interwoven and interdependent. The British government that would give up Malta would not remain in power for five minutes. Malta will only cease to form part of the British Empire when the Empire itself ceases to exist."**

When the Maltese revolted against the French on 2 September 1798 and ousted the French with the help of Britain, they asked to be taken under British protection, and the Treaty of Paris, which ended the war against France, placed Malta under the British flag.

War had always been a source of employment for the Maltese, especially since the Islands became a British base in 1800, when Malta served as a vital strategic post for Britain together with Gibraltar and Cyprus. It was not until the Treaty of Paris was signed, in 1814 that the Islands were officially declared as belonging *"in full right and sovereignty to his Britannic Majesty"*. The British Military Base was closed in 1979.

The prosperity that war brought to the Islands was evident with many Allied ships using the Maltese harbour. The British era saw various Governors trying to assist by initiating public works and encouraging emigration as a means of controlling the already dense population that was too large to be self-supporting. Under British rule many reforms were introduced such as abolition of monopolies in food supplies, the start of new industries and the introduction of a trial by jury.

The Maltese wanted to play a major role in the administration of the islands but this greater voice in the administration was not satisfied until 1887 when the Maltese elected representatives in the Council of Government could exercise some degree of self-governance. The changes introduced in 1887 functioned well for a time, but difficulties over the language question led the British Governor to withdraw the 1887 arrangement. In the face of great opposition to this, the British proposed Reforms, but the outbreak of the First World War shelved the idea.

The countries of the British Empire involved in the First World War hailed from Africa, Atlantic Islands, Australasia and Pacific Ocean, America, Asia, Europe, Indian Empire, Indian Ocean Islands, Middle East and the West Indies. British European colonies were Cyprus and Malta whilst Britain's two main naval stations in the Mediterranean were Gibraltar and Malta. The Allied powers were Great Britain, Russia, France, Italy, United States, and Japan. The Central Powers were Germany, Austria-Hungary and Turkey.

The strategic position of Malta and the military construction projects undertaken by the British placed Malta under the focus of attention. The opening of the Suez Canal made the Mediterranean more important than ever before as a coaling station on the imperial route to India and the Far East and a strategic naval base in the Mediterranean. Some of the most important war-related works were:

- Many public works for the encouragement of trade and industry
- Improvements in the Grand Harbour to make it more attractive to shipping.
- A new dock was opened by the Royal Navy in 1848.
- Harbour extensions at Marsa in 1859 and 1864–1865.
- More reliable water supply.
- A new Royal Navy dock in 1871 known as the 'Somerset' or Number 3 Dock at Senglea.
- A new hydraulic dock was built in 1873.
- The building of a breakwater in 1904, considered as the biggest work of all.
- The building of the only British warship in Malta, HMS *Melita*, launched in 1888.

The New Dock 1867

These projects are indicative of Malta's growth into a major transhipment hub in the middle of the Mediterranean. The British Empire required coal to keep it growing and Malta was transformed into a major link that fed a vast Empire.

The breakwater

It is also noted that from the beginning of the 20th Century, the coastal defences of Malta had been perfected and the strength of the Royal Navy was complete, so much so that Malta's defences were never tested or brought to action.

According to the *Daily Mirror Headlines*: The Battle of Ypres, published of 24 April 1915, on the Eastern Mediterranean, *"the importance of Malta cannot be over-estimated. Both the English and French fleets and transports are based on it – over 100 French ships and an even larger number of British"*.

1.6   Mobilisation of Maltese personnel

Ninety years ago, by *Proclamations XIV and VIII* of 5, August 1914, the Maltese fortress was mobilised and martial law was proclaimed. The two Battalions of the King's Own Malta Regiment of Militia were mobilised and marched to the coast of Malta and Gozo.[3]

**Proclamation
5 August, 1914**

On 3 August 1914, a proclamation was published directing the Royal Naval Reserve to be called into actual service and placing

---

3   For a detailed presentation of the role of the Maltese military regiments see Chapter 3 of this book.

the volunteers at the disposal of the Admiralty. Three days later, on the 6 August, the King's Own Malta Regiment and the Royal Engineers (Militia) Malta divisions were ordered to assemble.

The following morning, the whole regiment reported for service. When the call for the Naval Reserve was issued, hundreds volunteered for enlistment in the Navy and 300 were eventually chosen, increasing the existing force to 700. By the end of September, 1,000 Maltese were serving with the British fleet. On the 25 September, a movement was started for a Maltese battalion to offer their services for Lord Kitcheners's New Army for the front. During the day 200 pledged enlistments and by the first week of October, the number reached 1,000.

In the beginning of the New Year the Army Council informed the Malta Government that it had no use for these volunteers. The Governor of Malta asked the General Officer commanding Egypt, if he would make use of them but the latter replied that he had no

On the 14 January 1915, it was announced that the KOMRM had volunteered for foreign service and the First Battalion and a detachment of the Second Battalion under Lieutenant Colonel Charles B. Sciortino sailed for Cyprus. (See also Chapter 3 for the overseas service record of both the KOMRM and the RMA)

Maltese Troops in Cyprus. The group photo above shows Maltese officers of the KOMRM in a relaxed pose in Cyprus. At the far end of the right (standing) is Robert Samut (medical doctor). Robert Samut was the composer of the National Anthem L'Innu Malti. Seated (fourth from left) is Lieutenant-Colonel Charles B. Sciortino

(Photos by courtesy of Mr Andrew Cauchi)

use for untrained men. In March 1915, in the House of Commons, Colonel Yate M.P. urged that it was necessary to give a chance to Maltese and Cypriots to share in the Imperial defence. The Maltese militia and artillery both ought, he urged, be given a turn at the front.

In June 1915, the Governor of Malta proposed a detachment of 500 officers and men from the King's Own Malta Regiment of Militia be sent to join the Expeditionary Force in the Dardanelles. The Governor proposed that while away from Malta on service, the Maltese would be paid the same rates and given the same conditions as British territorial units doing the same work. The scheme was not approved for financial reasons.

Maltese cooks with British personnel on a Naval Ship
(Photo from a private collection)

A list of Italians who were married to Maltese ladies lost their lives at the Battle of Jutland in May 1916, whilst serving on different battleships (HMS *Defence* and HMS *Indefatigable*) that were sunk was given in a historical publication in 1922. Many Maltese also lost their lives as well. Many of the Italians who lost their lives were Bandsmen on the following ships:[4]

HMS *Defence*

Bandmaster: **Virgilio di Mauro**

Band's Corporal: **Nicola Foudacaro**

Bandsmen: **Gugliermo Rinaldi, Corado Muscara, Roberto Ventura, Giovanni Consiglio, Antonio Polato, Nunzio Carmando, Agostino Cavaliazzi, Emmanuele Ligroti**

4   *Il-Gbira Guerra tad-Dinja, Vol. III*, Opra Colossali li tigbor fiha l-ahjar fattijet tal guerra mehuda minn fuk cotba ta potenzi nuetrali Propieta' Letteraria u Artistica ta Andolfo & Magro, Stamperija u Legatorija ta' Emilio Lombardi, 28, Strada Santa Maria, u 27, 28, Strada San Trofimo Sliema (1922). pp.158–163

A fund-raising concert was organised on 11 November 1916 at 3.30 pm by a committee of Italian ladies service set up to help the families of Italian citizens who had been called up for military service and recruited in Malta. This was held at the Manoel Theatre under the auspices of the Governor and Lady Methuen and also the Consul

General of Italy and Signora De Lucchi. This programme was kindly made available by courtesy of Mr Winston Zammit, B.A (Hons), M.A.

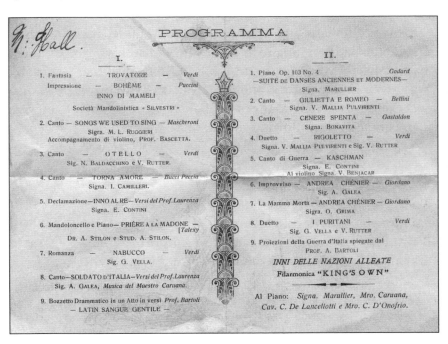

PROGRAMMA

I.

1. Fantasia — TROVATORE — Verdi
   Impressione — BOHÈME — Puccini
   INNO DI MAMELI
   Società Mandolinistica « SILVESTRI »

2. Canto — SONGS WE USED TO SING — Mascheroni
   Sigra. M. L. RUGGIERI
   Accompagnamento di violino, PROF. BASCETTA.

3. Canto — OTELLO — Verdi
   Sig. N. BALDACCHINO e V. RUTTER.

4. Canto — TORNA AMORE — Bucci Peccia
   Signa. I. CAMILLERI.

5. Declamazione—INNO AL RE—Versi del Prof.Laurenza
   Signa. E. CONTINI

6. Mandoloncello e Piano— PRIÉRE À LA MADONE —
   [Talexy
   DR. A. STILON e STUD. A. STILON.

7. Romanza — NABUCCO — Verdi
   Sig. G. VELLA.

8. Canto—SOLDATO D'ITALIA—Versi del Prof.Laurenza
   Sig. A. GALEA, Musica del Maestro Caruana.

9. Bozzetto Drammatico in un Atto in versi Prof. Bartoli
   — LATIN SANGUE GENTILE —

II.

1. Piano Op. 103 No. 4 — Godard
   —SUITE DE DANSES ANCIENNES ET MODERNES—
   Signa. MARULLIER

2. Canto — GIULIETTA E ROMEO — Bellini
   Signa. V. MALLIA PULVIRENTI

3. Canto — CENERE SPENTA — Gastaldon
   Signa. BONAVITA

4. Duetto — RIGOLETTO — Verdi
   Signa. V. MALLIA PULVIRENTI e Sig. V. RUTTER

5. Canto di Guerra — KASCHMAN
   Signa. E. CONTINI
   Al violino Signa. V. BENJACAR

6. Improvviso — ANDREA CHÉNIER — Giordano
   Sig. A. GALEA

7. La Mamma Morta — ANDREA CHÉNIER — Giordano
   Signa. O. GRIMA

8. Duetto — I PURITANI — Verdi
   Sig. G. VELLA e V. RUTTER

9. Proiezioni della Guerra d'Italia spiegate dal
   PROF. A. BARTOLI

INNI DELLE NAZIONI ALLEATE
Filarmonica "KING'S OWN"

Al Piano: Signa. Marullier, Mro. Caruana,
Cav. C. De Lanceliotti e Mro. C. D'Onofrio.

HMS *Indefatigable*

Bandmaster: **Enrico Portoghese**

Bandsmen: **Costantino Giunta, Achille Pollizzi, Giuseppe Portoghese, Archimede Priori, Matteo Rosmondo, Domenico Strano, Giovanni Urso**

On 11 August, 1915 the Inspector General of Communications of the Mediterranean Expeditionary Force reported to the Commander in Chief Malta: *'We urgently need 1,000 men for stevedore work on the beaches of the (Dardanelles) peninsula at once, possibly under fire, 'can help'?)*

Although employment in the dockyard, the military workshops, etc., was not lacking, about 1,200 volunteered to join the labour corps. They were paid 2s 6d a day as stevedores and 4s a day as gangers. From these 864 were selected and on 1 September 1915 sailed for Mudros.

Maltese troops parading

Some difficulty was met in maintaining discipline owing to lack of staff and to the presence of a number of 'loafers' and some 'bad characters' in the contingent. Groups of 70 a month were still sent from Malta as replacement for invalids, medically unfit and 'bad characters'. From the original group, 55 'useless and insubordinate' men were sent back at once and 247 poor workers and 'complaint makers' sent back after two months. The rest did useful work loading and unloading cargo, blasting, laying roads, cutting stone and wood, digging wells and stevedore work at ANZAC, Hellas, and Suvla beaches in the Dardanelles where 478 worked and at Mudros. Casualties during the first three months were one dead from wounds received and six wounded.

On 15 August the War Office asked for two more labour battalions, one of stevedores and one of labourers, for employment at Salonika, in Greece. On the 4th and 5th of September 300 stevedores and 400 labourers were enrolled. Another 100 labourers were recruited from Gozo. The contingent contained a number of Maltese officers and priests. The men were all subject to military law. In February 1917, the number of Maltese serving was substantial, considering the size of the island. Five officers and 42 men from the Royal Malta Artillery and several militia officers were with the 1,108 Maltese in Gallipoli and the 1,300 in Salonika. Seventy-five other officers were in the British services outside Malta and 300 officers and men with Canadian and Australian armed forces.

When further plans for the employment abroad of Maltese soldiers were mooted, the number of volunteers was disappointing, mainly because the British authorities would not pay them the same rates of British soldiers. Also calls for volunteers by the Army Service Corps, the Air Service and the Navy offered better terms and these were naturally preferred. On top of this was the fact that the Maltese people had been seeing the terrible state of the Allied sick and wounded brought to Malta from the Dardanelles. The reality of war was driven home and replaced the blind enthusiasm

British troops marching near the Main Guard, Valletta with Marich & Co. tobacconists shop in the background. Marich and Co. was established in 1838 and was the supplier of cigarettes to Naval and Military messes and clubs. Cousis and Marich were amongst the most popular cigarette brands with the troops

of the opening days when volunteers flocked to the colours. Despite all this, about 24,000 Maltese joined the various British services during the war.[5]

The Church and the civil and military authorities organised meetings and demonstrations to direct the population towards the war effort. In the process they were also explaining to the people the *raison d'etre* behind the war and the justification of its continuation by Britain and its allies

On the second anniversary since the commencement of hostilities, the Church, and the Governments over Europe held meetings to mark this occasion. In Malta a meeting was held at the

5   Information about mobilisation of Maltese servicemen has been kindly made available by courtesy of Mr Louis Henwood.

Floriana Granaries on 3 August 1916 at 4.30pm.[6] As preparation for the meeting, an appeal was made for all the population to attend and many large posters giving a clear indication of the programme, were fixed all around Malta. The meeting was addressed by the Governor and by the Archbishop and other prominent personalities.

The general Maltese sentiment for this meeting was that it was not right that demonstrations are held in furtherance of the war while others were of the opinion that the Ecclesiastical authorities should not take part such meetings. But when the meeting took place, and the people heard the speeches of the Archbishop and the Governor, the attitude of the people changed greatly as the theme of their speeches did not smack of vengeance. The demonstration took the tone of conciliation and reparation so that the generations to come would live in peace and justice.

The cream of the civil, military and naval establishments in Malta attended. As was announced in a local newspaper, the meeting started in time and was opened by the Governor's speech. He expressed his satisfaction that people attended in such a large number and also their approval of Britain's resolve for the continuation of war in order that liberty and justice would reign in the countries involved in the conflict. He praised the Maltese for their loyalty towards the British Empire and for their assistance in past conflicts where several Maltese lost their lives such as those in Africa and Egypt.

The Governor drew comparisons between the Great War and other conflicts in which Britain was involved during the 18th and the beginning of the 20th Centuries. He commented on Napoleon as a very ruthless man, but at the same time praised him for his

6   Il-Gbira Guerra tad-Dinja, Vol. III, Opra Colossali li tigbor fiha l-ahjar fattijet tal guerra mehuda minn fuk cotba ta potenzi nuetrali Propieta' Letteraria u Artistica ta Andolfo & Magro, Stamperija u Legatorija ta' Emilio Lombardi, 28, Strada Santa Maria, u 27, 28, Strada San Trofimo Sliema (1922).pp. 256–263

vision and intelligence, noting that he never used force against women, children or the elderly (as was being manifested during the Great War).

The Archbishop delivered his speech in Italian. He continued to stress the need that the war be won by the Britain and its allies. Only this could liberty and justice for all nations be guaranteed. He denounced Germany's policy of superiority over other nations and augured that peace might reign soon.

As soon as the speech was concluded, Mr Cicc. Azzopardi, President of the meeting's organizing committee summarised and translated into the Maltese language the Governor and Archbishop's speeches. The demonstration proceeded from Floriana to Valetta with the participation of 12 local village bands.

CHAPTER 2

GALLIPOLI

2.1 The Gallipoli Campaign

On the outbreak of the war, the British defence in the Mediterranean was inextricably linked to the protection of the Suez Canal. The Royal Navy guarded the approach to the canal to provide the necessary firepower in the event of an attack. It would have taken only one sunk vessel to block this vital passageway, which was the lifeline of Britain to the rest of its empire in India and the East.

When the Turkish army attacked in January 1915, they were quickly beaten off and more than 70,000 were amassed around the Suez Canal. The Gallipoli campaign tied down the Turkish approaches, which would have otherwise turned their attention against Egypt.

In April 1915, the Gallipoli peninsula witnessed one of the bloodiest landings ever recorded in battle history. It was the most infamous holocaust the world had ever known. The allies were represented by troops who included British, Australians, New Zealanders, Indians and Canadians, plus French colonial soldiers. The Maltese suffered a number of casualties while serving with British regiments and also seamen in the warships.

The growing power of the coastal defences made the amphibious assault at Gallipoli the more difficult and naval power ineffective. The main amphibious assault of the war occurred in the Dardanelles in 1915. It was hoped that the force of largely old pre-dreadnought battleships might force its way through to Constantinople to knock Turkey out of the war. This failed due to the guns and mines of the Turks. A campaign by Allied ground forces to capture the

Gallipoli patients recovering at Cottonera military hospital.
(Courtesy of Dr Charles Boffa)

straits and assist the passage of the fleet met with little success. The only successful part of the disaster was the withdrawal of the land forces by sea in early 1916.

Malta played a significant part in the Gallipoli campaign, not only as a back up base for the Royal Navy but also as one of the major hospitals and convalescent centres in the Mediterranean that looked after 58,000 servicemen wounded during the Great War. During the 9-month campaign Malta provided the support base in providing several eminent consultants, nearly 1,000 nurses (including Maltese V.A.D's) in the treatment of the casualties of the Gallipoli and Salonika campaigns.

The number of serviceman buried in Malta is an indicator of

Malta's contribution to the Allied effort during this devastating war. There are 1500 British and 26 Anzac servicemen buried in Malta as well as French, Indians and Egyptians together with 26 Turkish prisoners.

The Dardanelles is a narrow strategic passage from the warm waters of the Mediterranean through the sea of Marmara, and from there through the even narrower Bosphorus to the Black sea, provides Russia's only year round ice free access to the world's oceans. This access was historically coveted by the Russians and a cause of the Crimean war. During the First World War it was to be the setting for a British amphibious operation of disastrous proportions.

The combined British, French, New Zealand and Australian troops landed at dawn on the 25 April 1915 along the dangerous coastline and there were welcomed with a devastating resistance by the Turkish army who were well positioned on the hillside. The landing took place on the eastern side as part of an operation involving 75,000 troops. The plans went wrong with the force landing a mile north, and instead of finding an open plane they found themselves facing steeply rising ridges and gorges. Total surprise was lost and the troops found themselves facing murderous fire.

2.2   Charles Bonavia

Several Maltese/Australians, including Charles Bonavia, fought side by side with the Australian troops. Bonavia was born in Malta in 1888 and his father was the Registrar at the Malta Law Courts and his grandfather rose to the rank of Colonel in the Royal Malta Fencible Artillery. Bonavia studied architecture at the University of Malta and migrated to Australia.

He joined the 11ᵗʰ Battalion 3ʳᵈ Infantry Brigade and sailed with his regiment from Fremnantle to Egypt on 2 November 1914. Bonavia's name is included in the list of the fallen soldiers who died

Cape Helles beach

Gallipoli Coast looking north from Cape Helles

at Anzac Cove at Line Pine and also at the National war Memorial in Canberra. Other Maltese whose names are forever recorded at Helles Memorial overlooking Dardanelles are Major Herbert Sammut who died when he was in command of Essex Regiment and Lieutenant Herbert Huber. Huber was a member of the Royal Iniskilling Fusiliers and was killed few hours before the British forces successfully evacuated from the Turkish soil. Unfortunately, their remains were never discovered.

Many other Maltese migrants were among the casualties at Gallipoli. According to John Anthony Mizzi, there were many Maltese migrants were among the casualties at Gallipoli. According to John Mizzi, there were 800 Maltese labourers serving under Maltese officers in Gallipoli. The early Maltese settlers gave an important contribution in the preservation of freedom and democracy.[1]

2.3   Malta-related episodes

An organisation was set up in March 1915 to deal with the problems of mines. The damage to the French squadron had been severe: *Gaulois* had been forced to ground herself on Rabbit Island to the north of Tenedos, and the *Suffren* was leaking from the effects of a plunging shell. The *Gaulois*, however, was soon pumped out and refloated, and with the *Inflexible* and the *Suffren* she went off to Malta for repairs.

Meanwhile the organisation of the new minesweeping force began. One hundred and fifteen men from the trawler crews were sent home and there was an overwhelming response from the crews of the *Ocean* and the *Irresistible* for volunteers to replace them. Kites, wire mesh, and other tackle were ordered from Malta,

---

1   See also, *Gallipoli: The Malta Connection*, John A. Mizzi, 1991

and at Tenedos, Greek fishermen were engaged to help the British crews in equipping the destroyers as minesweepers.

Transport ships carrying the 29th Division en route to Gallipoli (as reinforcements) arrived at Malta during March 1915 and the officers were entertained at a special performance of the Opera *Faust*.

During April, the Royal Navy had been extremely busy with a number of improvisations. Three dummy battleships were constructed. These were ordinary merchantmen enlarged and disguised with wooden guns and superstructure. From a distance the silhouette they presented was exactly that of a battleship, and it was hoped that their presence in the Aegean might induce the German Fleet to come out and fight in the North Sea. One of them was subsequently torpedoed by a U-boat near Malta, and must have occasioned some surprise to the Germans, as the ship settled her wooden turrets and her 12-inch guns gloated away on the tide.

A British submarine *E11* under the command of captain, Lieut.-Commander Nasmith, spread terror through the Sea of Marmara during May 1915 sinking ship after ship in the approaches to the Golden Horn, for it was thought that at least half a dozen submarines were operating in the area. This submarine eventually sailed to Malta for repairs after a serious defect developed in the port main motor and the starboard intermediate shaft cracked.

In May and June, there was a plague of flies that was persistent and horrible more than the war itself. The flies fed on the unburied dead and on the latrines and refuse of food of both armies. No tin of food could be opened without being covered instantly with a thick layer of writhing insects. Mosquito nets were almost unknown.

From June onwards dysenteric diarrhoea spread through the Army and soon every man was infected by it. The medical services came near to break down during as they had been organised on the principle that hospitals would be set on the peninsula soon after the original landing. When this failed to happen, hurried arrangements were made to establish a base under canvas on the island of Lemnos, while more serious cases were evacuated to Egypt, Malta and even England. The increasing number of casualties soon overwhelmed Lemnos and there were never enough hospital ships to cope with the overflow.

2.4   Maltese Servicemen in Greece

France and Britain brought Greece into the war in 1917 against the wishes of the King of Greece. Britain and France sent a military expedition to Salonika in October 1915 and then attempted to coerce the pro-German King Constantine into war on the allied

This rare photograph shows Maltese servicemen of the King's Own Malta Regiment of Militia who in 1915 volunteered for service in Salonika (Greece). They are seen together with Greek children and other Greek folk in traditional dress. The first serviceman on the right is Arthur (k/aTuru) Grech who is the grandfather of Arthur (Turu) Grech of Sliema whose antiques shop is situated at Manwel Dimech in Sliema, close to the Police Station.
Photo by courtesy of Mr Arthur Grech

side. Although not as blatant as German aggression in Belgium, it was another violation of the rights of small nations.[2]

2.5   ANZAC Day

Some 50,000 members of the Australian Imperial forces from a total Australian population of just 5 million served at Gallipoli and more than 8,700 Australian and 2,700 New Zealanders were killed during the campaign

On 25 April of every year, Australia commemorates the anniversary of Anzac day when the Australian and New Zealanders landed on the beaches of Gallipoli. This day is also commemorated overseas in the main at Anzac Cove (Gallipoli – Turkey). This day commemorates the Australians and New Zealanders who died in action at Gallipoli in 1915 and in subsequent military actions.

An annual ANZAC Day commemoration ceremony has been held in Malta since 1916. The presence in Malta of New Zealand Airmen in 1952, gave the local commemoration a special significance and as from 1954, the commemoration became more impressive.

Present for the ceremony in 1954, was Captain J.L. Muscat who had been in charge of some 200 members of the Malta Labour Corps serving at ANZAC sector on Gallipoli. It is interesting to note that this unit lost only one man, 27 year old Labourer 913, Giuseppe Camilleri, through its service there. Camilleri lost his life during a Turkish bombardment on December 7, 1915 and is buried at Ari Burnu Cemetery on Gallipoli. He was the son of Angelo and Filippa Camilleri of Sliema.[3]

---

2   *The Collins History of the World in the Twentieth Century*, J.A.S Grenville, 1994, p.99

3   *Sunday Times (Malta)* 25 April 2004. pp.50–51

A new ANZAC service was held for the first time in Malta as part of the ceremonies to mark the 89th anniversary of ANZAC Day on 25 April 2004. This dawn service was held at the Mtarfa Military Cemetery near Ta' Qali at 5.30 a.m. An ecumenical service and wreath-laying ceremony (as is the tradition in Malta) was later held at the Pietà Military Cemetery.[4]

---

4   *Times (Malta)* 26 April 2004. p.48

CHAPTER 3

THE ROYAL MALTA ARTILLERY (RMA) AND THE KING'S OWN MALTA REGIMENT OF MILITIA (KOMRM)

Note: See Appendix A for a list of Maltese Officers and men who served in the RMA and KOMRM during the First World War.

The local defence was principally entrusted to the officers and men of the RMA and two Battalions of the KOMRM, with strength of 1,032 and 3,393 respectively. There were also the Garrison Battalions of the West Kent Regiment and of the Northumberland Fusiliers, and for a time, two London Regiments that were in Malta principally for training purposes.[1]

Although during the first World War, Malta was not attacked or ran the risk of an invasion due to the overwhelming British and French naval force in comparison to the German Imperial Navy, the defence of the islands was also given due importance and several shore and inland fortifications were updated with better armaments. More Maltese recruits were taken to serve in the army and supporting services.

Having established themselves in Malta, the British developed and built defences on the island to keep the island defended with state of the art weaponry until the late 1950s. Around 30 forts were built between 1860 and 1938. It was only after 1850 that they felt the need to embark on an extensive programme of re-armament

1   Fifty-two battalions of the Northumberland Fusiliers were formed in the Great War. They were in action from the first day at Mons, and the battle honours, Ypres, 1914, '15, '17 and '18, "tells its own tale". The regiment was also represented gallantly in Italy, Salonika and Gallipoli. As a result of its splendid service, the prefix "Royal" was bestowed on the regiment.

and fortress building. Thus, started the fortress 'building boom' of the 1870s, '80s and '90s. By 1900, the British army in Malta was capable of defending the harbours and dockyards even when the fleet was away. The process of arming and re-arming the forts of Malta was a continuous one, and only ended at the end of the 1950s, when coast artillery was abandoned as a result of the introduction of guided weapons. Unlike the fortifications of the Knights, the British fortifications were intentionally designed to blend in with the countryside, and are therefore far less evident than the bastions around Malta's cities as they are low lying (built low in the ground.[2]

3.1 Royal Malta Artillery (RMA)

During the Great War about 20,000 Maltese joined the Empire forces. The RMA's strength in 1914 was of 22 officers and 3,421 other ranks. On the outbreak of the war, the Regiment was already at its war stations and the reservists were called back to the colours.

When Germany invaded Belgium and France and the regular troops, ammunition and guns stationed Malta were sent overseas to European battlefields, the territorials took over the defence of the islands; two Battalions of the KOMRM were mobilised.

The garrison artillery consisted of 8 companies plus the RMA that manned the Coast Defence Forts with 16, 9.2-inch guns, 14, 6-inch guns and 12, 15-pounders.[3]

In November 1914, a fourth company was formed. It took over some forts previously manned by a company of the Royal Garrison Artillery. The RMA also manned other guns such as the 10-inch rifled muzzle loaded guns at *Għargħur* and 3-pouunder anti-air

---

2   *Times of Malta*, Tuesday, February 10, 2004, feature titled 'Fortress bulding by the British in Malta', subject of DLH lecture. pp32–33.

3   *Britain in the Mediterranean & the defence of her naval stations*, Quentin Hughes, 1981.

craft equipment on St James Cavalier in Valletta. At the beginning of the war the island's northern bays were undefended, so a new battery was hastily constructed at *Wardija* overlooking St Paul's Bay and armed with two 6-inch guns, which were dismantled from *Wolseley Battery* at *Delimara*.

The development of the machine gun as a means of defence changed the defensive strategy during the First World War. The concept of coastal defences took on a new design in that coastal forts defended by ditches and bastions was changed to earth works, low in profile and heavily protected by barbed wire and heavy machine gun fire.[4]

In 1915 several officers volunteered for service overseas and were posted to units of the British Expeditionary Forces in France, Gallipoli and Egypt. In the same year a number of other ranks responded to a call for volunteers by the Royal Navy Ordnance Depot at the, then HM Dockyard. An explosion in the ammunition yard in October 1915 caused a number of casualties, including 14 Maltese soldiers killed.

In 1916, a detachment under Major E. Savona joined the Egyptian Expeditionary Force and manned the coast defences in Egypt. They returned after the Armistice.

In 1917, one officer and three NSO's recruited British subjects in Tunis and Tripoli. In 1918, a fifth company was formed and the existing companies were increased to regimental establishment of 890 officers and other ranks, excluding personnel, overseas. At the end of hostilities the regiment was employed in guarding prisoners of war at Fort Manoel and Polverista Barracks until March 1920 when it returned to its peacetime barracks at St Elmo and Lascaris.

---

4   *The British Fortifications, An Illustrated Guide to the British Fortifications in Malta*, Stephen C. Spiteri, p. 12, 1991.

3.2   King's Own Malta Regiment of Militia (KOMRM)

On 14 January 1915, it was announced that the KOMRM had volunteered for foreign service and the First Battalion and a detachment of the Second Battalion under Lieutenant Colonel Charles Sciortino sailed for Cyprus, on garrison duties and a number of officers and men volunteered for service in Gallipoli and Salonika, while several offices served at the Western Front and other theatres with British line regiments.[5]

In September 1915, two RMA Subalterns and twelve Maltese Offices of the KOMRM besides 1,000 Maltese Labourers under the Command of Major Aspinal KOMRM, were sent to the Dardanelles. The Officers of the KOMRM were the following:

Lieut. Herbert Huber who proceeded to the Dardanelles with his regiment. The KOMRM retuned to Malta in August 1915.

Second Lieut. Arthur Vella who went from Cyprus to Alexandria

Major Micallef Eynaud
Major Aspinal
Captain Frank Stivala
Lieut. Achille Dandria
Lieut. Charles Muscat
Lieut. Joseph Muscat
Lieut. Joseph Agius
Lieut. Leonard Sammut
Lieut. U. Von Brockdorff
Lieut. Edward Mifsud.

---

5   *Malta at War*, by John Anthony Mizzi and Mark Anthony Vella, volume I, pp. 58–59

Shortly before the evacuation *Lieut. Huber* of the KOMRM, attached to the Inniskilling was killed at Cape Helles on 7 January 1916, *Lieut. Alfred Micallef Eynaud* and *Lieut. Arthur Vella* were killed on other fronts.[6]

On the 5 December 1917, a second Battalion was sent to Salonika under the command of *Major Vella*, KOMRM. The other Officers from the KOMRM were:

Captain Charles Pace
Lieut. Edgar Huber (who was killed accidentally)
Lieut. S. Sammut Tagliaferro with the rank of Major succeeded *Major C. Vella* (who was invalid).

The Chaplains were *Father Bezzina* of the Dominican Order
Reverend Cauchi from Floriana

The Medical Officers were *Captain Vella* RASC and
Dr Paul Boffa RAMC (later Sir and Prime Minister of Malta).

On February 18 1918, a labour company under the command of A/*Captain Charles Brockdorff* KOMRM left for Salonika, consisting of 125 men; 200 others left on the 28th under A/*Captain W. Bonello*.

Lieut. Frank Gollcher was in charge of the Mining Company in Italy.

The KOMRM was also responsible as noted earlier, for outpost duty in the many of coastal towers around the coast of Malta and Gozo.

---

6   Thirteen Royal Inniskilling Fusiliers battalions were formed during the Great War and the Regiment was in action at Le Cateau and Mons.

Lieutenant G.F. Amato Gauci receiving the
Military Cross from his Excellency Viscount
Gort V.C. at the investiture (May 1943)

Maltese military family tradition has been very evident and a fine example of this is found under the heading of 'Malta's Second Investiture', the *Sunday Times of Malta* of May 30 1943, 'an admirer' wrote as follows on page 6:

> **"Lieutenant G.F. Amato-Gauci is upholding family traditions. He is the son of Major A. Amato-Gauci, late K.O.M.R and R.A.F and the grandson of the late Colonel Count P. Bernard, former Commanding Officer of the R.M.A. He is also a nephew of the late Colonel Sir Edgar Bernard, K.B.E. C.M.G., and of Colonel J. Bernard C.M.G. D.S.O. Two of his first cousins were killed in action in the last war and he has three brothers now serving, one a Major in the R.M.A. and the other two, captains in the K.O.M.R. Another brother was serving as Captain in the R.M.A. at the time of his death".[7]**

---

7   See also Appendix A of this book for Amato-Gauci's service in the First World War.

CHAPTER 4

AVIATION

4.1 The first flight

Civil aviation developed over the past century. It was Orville Wright's historic 12-second flight on 17 December 1903 that started a take-off process in aviation that developed further in 1908 when Wilbur Wright operated a flight lasting just 29 seconds.

Subsequently commercial aviation began in 1914 from St Petersburg to Tampa in Florida on 1 January 1914. This was the first scheduled flight. On 11 March 1918 the world's first scheduled international airmail flight was operated between Vienna and Kiev.[1]

4.2 The Royal Air Force

The first years of the First World War saw the birth of the Royal Air Force. The Navy and the Military authorities of Britain combined their separate air forces known as Royal Naval Air Service and Royal Flying Corps respectively into one force. Hence the Royal Air Force was established officially through *The Air Force (Constitution) Bill*, which came into force on 1 April 1918.

The Royal Air Force came into existence at the most critical stage of the major German offensive in France. At the time, the Armistice was signed, it boasted of 200 squadrons with 3,300 first line aircraft. This epoch-making event was linked to three names, Smuts, Churchill and Trenchard. On 6 June 1918, an independent

---

1   See *Times (Malta)* of 23 December, p.7, 2003.

force was created under the command of Lord Trenchard (then Sir Hugh) for action against industrial centres of Germany. Up to the fatal armistice, the force dropped 550 tons of bombs. In a raid on Berlin 25 years after (1943) the R.A.F. had released 900 tons in less than one hour![2]

When Trenchard founded the R.A.F, as an independent service, he had to fight obstinate forces of reaction. The Army and the Navy both wanted to control the air. Parliament, thinking in terms of disarmament, had little cash to spare for this youthful upstart. But the dynamic resource of the new service overcame these obstacles.

4.3   Aviation in Malta

The birth of aviation in Malta is attributed to an Air Balloon Flight in 1904 when the Royal Engineers Balloon Unit visited Malta. The first page of Malta's aviation history was written on 13 February 1915 when a Short Seaplane Type 135 No. 136 performed its first flight in Malta taking-off from the surface of Grand Harbour's waters

Malta's Great War aviation history is indeed a chequered one. Malta proved its worth not only in the construction of World War One flying boats planes at the Dockyard but also in providing an invaluable sea base.

4.4   U-boat Detection

In World War One, the Navy flew escort for coastal convoys, searched for submarines and enemy vessels and patrolled the coastlines. Charged with the defence of the United Kingdom, the Navy pursued this with airships, balloons, aeroplanes and

---

2   See **Times of Malta**, Wednesday, 31 March 1943, under the heading '*Birth of the R.A.F. Today – World's Mightiest Air Force*'.

flying boats. When the Royal Air force was established, the naval contribution had included a large number of boats, essential to the operation of waterborne balloons and waterborne aircraft. These boats provided transport for servicing staff, ferrying supplies, and, of course towing the equivalent of the landplane requiring trucks and tractors for the same reasons.[3]

The U-boat Campaign of the German Imperial Navy, which was wrecking havoc of Merchant and Naval ships, put pressure on the Naval Authorities for a construction of a Sea Plane Base at Kalafrana and by May of 1916 a number of hangers and spillways were completed.

The role of the seaplane was to search and keep track of submarine routes. Marking the route and reporting their positions was fundamental information to be relayed to the Royal Navy. The work was quite in its initial and primitive stages. Due to the lack of advanced technology Air to Sea Vessel was based on human sight alone. Binoculars were the main instrument and detection depended also very heavily on calm seas that could indicate any foam or other patterns of a moving U-boat. Attempts were made to convert ships into plane carriers and the HMS *Ark Royal* was the first British naval ship to take aircraft in February 1915.

4.5   Balloons and Sea Plane Construction

Following the decision (late in 1915) to construct a new seaplane base for Malta, at Kalafrana, work began at once. Some materials originally intended for the construction of huts in the Dardanelles campaign were made available and a slipway and seaplane hangar were part of the scheme. At the end of July 1916 soon after completion of the new facilities, five Curtiss America flying boats

---

3   *Call-Out, A wartime diary of air/sea rescue operations at Malta*, Frederick R. Galea, , p8, 2002

arrived from Felixstowe, carrying seven flying officers, two warrant officers and number of mechanics, under the command of Flight Commander J.D. Maude.

In March 1917, three Short 184 seaplanes were sent out from Dundee in Scotland to replace the three remaining Curtiss Americas and, during June, two Italian-built FBA flying boats were added. One of these was forced to land on the sea in July after warning a convoy of the presence of enemy submarines about 45 miles south-east of the island. The flying boat then drifted onto the north coast of Africa and the crew was captured by Arab tribesmen.[4]

The Kalafrana sea base used for wartime activities is now no longer in existence as it has made way for an economic venture: the Freeport. A classical case of '*a sword turned into a ploughshare*'.

4.6   Manoel Island

In November 1917 a technical delegation arrived in Malta led by Wing Commander H. Delacombe in order to set up a Balloon Unit. Six sheds were constructed at the entrance to *Lazzarrett at Manoel Island*, Gzira each holding one Balloon. A gas-making plant was also constructed for filling the balloons.

4.7   HM Dockyard

The '*Unrestricted Submarine Warfare*' U-boat campaign of the German Imperial Navy placed huge demands on Britain for aircraft construction in the Central Mediterranean Region, so much so that Kalafrana was seen as the ideal base for operating such flights and the HM Dockyard Construction Unit had the best manpower and construction site for the sea planes. In all 23 planes

---

4   Ibid, p.295

The first Felixstowe F3 was constructed in November 1917 at the Dockyard

were constructed in Malta. With the setting up of the Royal Air Force, Maltese workers were recruited and up to August 1918, 700 were enrolled. A special training camp was set up at Spinola, St Julian's.

The seaplanes arrived in large crates in unassembled wooden parts. The assembly design map, lathes and other special material were also sent. The first Felixstowe type airplane F.3 (N4310) was completed in November 1917 and the model's design was based on the Curtiss H-4 America flying boats which were already operating from the Kalafrana base. This airplane was constructed as part of an order of 12 other planes of the same type, which by end November 1918 the order was finished (N4311-N4321). Another order for 38 planes was reduced to 11 (N4360-N4370) in view of the nearing of the end of hostilities.

At the end of the war the Malta Royal Air Force station was gradually reduced, commencing in the year 1919 and proceeding further in 1920, 1922 and 1923.

A crippled U-boat being pursued by a British Curtiss 'Large America' flying boats

4.8 Wyndlham Levy Grech (1890—1956) and other Maltese RAF personnel

Another important landmark in Maltese Aviation History was the first ever Maltese pilot who flew into combat during the First World War.

Born in 1889 in Pernambuco, Brazil, Grech was brought to Malta shortly after his birth together with his mother Terezina, and brought up by his Uncle Dr Oreste Grech Mifsud. He changed his surname from Levy-Grech to Grech.

Educated at St Ignatius College, St Julian's, Grech graduated in 1913 in Doctor of Laws and soon after the outbreak of hostilities in March 1916, he volunteered to join the Royal Flying Corps. He was successful in all his tests and was granted his aviator's certificate (number 7293 on 19 July 1916).

Mr Grech in RAF uniform

He was posted with 42 Squadron in France during August 1916 on the Western Front. On 11 September 1916 he shot down his first enemy aircraft and while flying a sortie his aircraft was hit by return fire. His air gunner was killed and Mr Grech was seriously wounded. Mr Grech was mentioned in several dispatches, subsequently receiving the Italian Government's title '*Cavaliere della Corona d'Italia*' on 1 April 1920. From 1921 to 1927 Grech served with the colonial services as an acting chief justice in the Seychell Islands.

During the Second World War, he was recalled to the RAF as Deputy Judge Advocate with the rank of Squadron Leader and as also mentioned in dispatches.[5]

In March, 1918, 778 Maltese enlisted in the Royal Air Force as A.C II for Foreign Service. Captain Attilio Amato Gauci. Lieut. Count Frank Sant Cassia and Lieut. Philip Manduca of the KOMR were also sent for disciplinary and training purposes.

5   See, also Maltese Biographies of the Twentieth Century, 1997, Edition, by Michael J. Schiavone and Louis J. Scerri, pp330–331 and Malta: An Aviation History by Aflred Coldman, pp.26–27, 2001.

At the time of the armistice, Maltese airmen were serving overseas at Otranto, Taranto, Brindisi, Stavros, Imbros, Corfu, Constantinople, Mudros and Alexandria, under the command of Lieut. Philip Manduca, OC Maltese RAF troops overseas.

Many Maltese officers volunteered for overseas service and some were killed. Eight were awarded the Military Cross and many were mentioned in dispatches.

4.9   Zeppelin Raid!

April 1918: A giant Zeppelin loaded with death and destruction took off from a German base in Bulgaria heading for an important allied naval base in the Mediterranean – Malta. Only the vulnerability of this weapon to the slightest accident saved the unsuspecting people of the island from their first air raid during the First World War.

The Zeppelin had already been used during the war and by the end of February 1918, *LZ 104* Airship attacked Naples on the West coast of Italy dropping over 56,000 kilos of bombs on the naval base and other important industrial establishments – with rather less effect than its commander Lt. Cmdr. Ludwig Bockholt claimed.

An attack on Port Said in Egypt on March 20, failed and could not be carried through as the airship met a very strong headwind. The same reason foiled an attempt to bomb the British naval base in the Bay of Suda on Crete.

April 7, 1918 saw *LZ 104* rising majestically from its base at Yambol in Bulgaria for the last time. This time the target was Malta and its important naval docks and facilities. The airship crossed the Balkan Peninsula and the straits of Toronto behind the heel of Italy. Then it disappeared.

The only witness was a German submarine (*UC 53*) cruising the coast of Italy. About 9.30 p.m. the watch lookouts on the surfaced U-boat observed light followed by a sea of flames that lit the horizon. A few seconds later the echo of an explosion rumbled through the Strait.

The U-boat investigated and found some oily patches and a few pieces of wreckage. Neither the Italians nor any other Allied Forces ever claimed to have brought down the airship. Filled with thousands of cubic metres of explosive hydrogen gas vulnerable to the least spark and some 5,000 kilos of bomb and incendiaries, *LZ 104* was truly a flying bomb. An accident brought down this airship and saved Malta from its first air raid.[6]

The Zeppelin

---

6   This story has been sourced from a *1978 publication titled Malta at War by Richard Muscat*. In this magazine, a selection of less known true stories of Malta at war is presented. The magazine was published by Joe Azzopardi, Marsa and printed by Progress Press Co. Ltd.

CHAPTER 5

MALTA DOCKYARD AND GRAND HARBOUR

5.1 The importance of the Dockyard

During the First World War Maltese industry had become synonymous with the naval dockyard, which was based in the creeks around the Three Cities, and which employed thousands of skilled and unskilled Maltese workers. The presence of the four navies in the Mediterranean, British, French, Japanese and Italian made great calls on the Dockyard where work went on night and day. Unemployment was inexistent.

During the Great War, the dockyards worked ceaselessly to maintain Allied shipping in fighting condition. The Malta Drydocks played an important contribution in the Allied victory during the Great War. The Admiralty had a great trust not only in the workers' skills and hard work, but also above all in their loyalty. Ship repair on war ships was much in demand.

Fleet in Grand Harbour

The Grand Harbour and its environs witnessed a continuous activity with many ships of different navies visiting Malta for repair and maintenance work and for provision replenishment. The Grand Harbour and the Dockyard workforce numbered 13,500 plus about 3,000 other workers involved in port handling and other ancillary services. This hub of activity resulted in an increase in trade especially in the Cottonera, Valletta and Floriana area.[1]

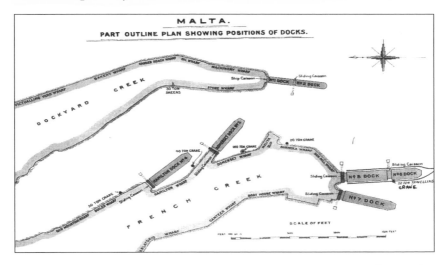

It is noted that during the Dardanelles campaign, the Malta Drydocks was the nearest docks and as a result much work was required overseas. Many Maltese workers were transferred to Corfu' to perform repair work.

---

1   See also *Malta's grand Harbour and its Environs in War and Peace*, Dr Charles J. Boffa, 2000

A landing barge brings 'jack' ashore at Grand Harbour.
In the background it is possible to see Saint Barbara Bastions and Sir Alexander
Ball's Monument at Lower Baracca Gardens

5.2   The workforce

The number of Maltese who served in connection with the Royal
Navy and naval establishments was rather over 15,900. It was
claimed for the Malta Dockyard that it worked at higher pressure
during the war than any dockyard outside the United Kingdom
and of the total, two-thirds, were labourers at the Dockyard
Naval Ordinance Depot and Victualling Yard. Nearly 2,400 were
employed in coaling; there were nearly 1,300 seagoing services,
200 engaged in minesweeping and 500 in labour parties at bases
away from Malta. The Royal Air Force employed 778 Maltese and
in all 31,739 men voluntarily served the Government in Malta
and overseas. Submarine perils did not prevent 630 Maltese from
taking engagements in Mercantile Marine during the war against
an average of 200 in normal times.

The truth of the above was borne out not only by Mr Lloyd George, the British Prime Minister, by Admiral Carden, the Commander-in Chief of the Allied Fleets who in a dispatch of the 17 March 1915 drew the attention of the Lords of the Admiralty, '*to the excellent work done by the Malta Dockyard*', but also by Rear-Admiral Ballard, who, as the Admiral Superintendent of the yard during a very critical part of the war, was in a the best position to express an opinion on the subject.

In the course of a lecture given at the University of Malta on 7 November 1917, he described an interview he had with the First Sea Lord in the previous July on receiving orders to relieve Rear Admiral Limpus, whose term of office was about to expire:

> **"The First Lord informed me that war activity was at a higher pressure in Malta than in any other place outside the United Kingdom. Malta, he added, is a vital part of the line of communications, allied troopships and war-vessels, (800 per month) are passing through the island, numberless hospital ships carry thousands of sick and wounded thereto, allied merchant ships are working at high pressure day and night and about 15,000 tons of coal are being handled week by week."**

5.3   Ordnance Stores (*Polverista*)

During 1902, the Naval Ordnance Department was set up and the Royal Navy continued with the programme of excavation works for new stores and also the enlargement of other stores. This Department also made use of the stores that were used by the Order of St John in 1756.

The Royal Navy during the First World War used these stores in that they supplied the whole Mediterranean Fleet. In all over 400,000 shells, 7,000 depth charges and 73,000 hand grenades were supplied as war material from these stores. Thousands of grenades were produced at these stores.[2]

5.4   Explosion at Ordnance Stores

In June 1915 Sir Ian Hamilton, commander at the Dardanelles required a large quantity of hand grenades and asked the Malta government to help. In a short time Maltese workers under British supervision manufactured and dispatched 68,112 hand grenades to the Dardanelles.

The shortage of grenades brought much work to the Maltese, especially during the Gallipoli campaign. A foundry in Ħamrun forged these grenades at Pace's foundry, whilst men of the Royal Malta Artillery volunteered to fill the grenades with gun cotton and a brass plug as a seal. 50 men in all commenced the work at a laboratory within the HM Dockyard in August 1915 at the Naval Ordnance Department of H M. Dockyard. Disaster struck on October 5 when a stack of over 100 grenades accidentally blew up killing 14 Maltese soldiers and wounding 15 others. The explosion took place in one of the tents occupied by some fifty men of the Royal Malta Artillery who were engaged in filling hand grenades.

Every assistance was rendered immediately by the men in the Dockyard, seamen from the ships lying in the Creek, and by French sailors. A Chaplain belonging to the French Navy administered the last rites to the dying. The injured men were taken to the Bighi Royal Naval Hospital. This incident was not given much publicity during the time because of the unrestricted submarine warfare that indiscriminately attacked Allied and suspicious neutral shipping, both military and merchant with torpedoes as well as ships carrying thousands of sick and wounded treated in Malta. In fact, one of the soldiers who was awarded the silver Life Saving

2   *L-Istorja tat-Tarzna*, Karmenu Ellul Galea, 1973

Medal of the venerable Order of St John was only given this after the end of the war.[3]

The Maltese soldiers were buried at Rinella Cemetery in Kalkara where the Royal Navy has erected a memorial over their graves. One of the names is that of Gunner Guiseppe Bonnici, 28 years old who is the grandfather of Mr Louis Henwood's wife.[4]

Two victims of the Explosion at Ordnance Stores

Gunner Francesco Grixti   **Gunner Giuseppe Bonnici**

(Another important assignment for Drydocks workers during the war was the construction of seaplanes at the Boat House. These planes were made of wood) – See also (Chapter 4: Aviation).

---

3   See, *Times of Malta*, Friday October 2, p8 1998 . Letter to the Editor by John .A. Mizzi titled The Gallipoli campaign. Mr Mizzi is also the author of '*Gallipoli – the Malta Connection*', 1991

4   Photo and information about Gunner Giuseppe Bonnici by kind permission of Mr Louis Henwood who has also a page on the internet dedicated to Mr Bonnici *at http://louishenwood.com/history/no29.html*

List of Ordnance Stores explosion victims
(Buried in The Roman Catholic Naval Cemetery at Rinella)

Reg. No.		Born at	Date of Enlistment/Age	Grave No.
1350	Carmelo Farrugia	Xewkija	13 May, 1890 (21)	104
1571	Gio Batta Dalli	Birkirkara	14 Mar, 1895 (18)	91
2659	Carmelo Gauci	Naxxar	10 Mar, 1904 (24)	103
2683	Paolo Xerri	Qormi	11 Jul, 1904 (18)	101
2688	Giuseppe Bonnici	Safi	28 Jul, 1903 (18)	97
2837	Francesco Grixti	Gudja	4 Mar 1909 (21)	94
2849	Giuseppe Tanti	Dingli.		100

He had first joined the RMA, aged 18 on 1ˢᵗ June 1902 and was allotted Regimental No 2579, but was discharged at his own request on payment of £12 after serving 1 year and 140 days in the Regiment. He rejoined on 14 July 1909.

2876	Pietro Caruana	Qrendi	22 Mar, 1910 (22)	92
2879	Giovanni Demicoli	Birkirkara	8 Jun, 1910 (20)	98
2911	Giuseppe Gafa'	Msida	23 Nov, 1910 (19)	99
2934	Giuseppe Borg	Mqabba	31 Mar, 1911 (18)	95
2963	Lucrezio Calleja	Birkirkara	7 Dec, 1911 (18)	102
2965	Francesco Farrugia	Qrendi	7 Dec, 1911 (19)	96
3193	Fedele Barbara	Safi.		93

He had first joined the RMA, aged 18 years on 22 February 1901 and was allotted Regimental No. 2428. He was discharged on termination of his period of engagement on 21 February 1913. He rejoined the

Regiment on 18 May 1915 and, met his tragic death merely 141 days after that date.[5]

5.5   French Navy

During the war, the French Navy was based in Maltese waters and many French ships required repair and maintenance at the Docks. Winston S. Churchill who was the First Lord of the Admiralty invited the French Navy to use the Maltese harbours as they would Toulon.

The craftsmanship of the Maltese workers was epitomized by the geniality of Mr Salvu Mallia, an engine-fitter from Vittoriosa, who managed to discover and develop a formula at the Tool Room to adjust lathes for the French measure. As most of the equipment at the Docks was programmed for Imperial measures, the spiral ridge to cut a French screw required 127 ridges on the tread cutter as against 129 for the Imperial measure. Mr Mallia's dexterity solved this problem.

5.6   HMS *Melita*

Between 1882 and 1888, six Mariner class composite screw sloops were built. HMS *Melita* was one of these ships and it was the only British warship built in Malta. The Melita was launched in 1888.

According to *The Graphic*, Illustrated Weekly Newspaper of London dated 14 April 1888, the British wanted to put to use the HM Dockyard facilities when the Navy was away from the Island. This was also an experimental decision taken to build Melita

---

5   List and details made available by permission and courtesy of Mr Andrew Cauchi.
Francesco Grixti RMA was present for the Coronation of King George V in 1911. His brother was the first Superior of the M.U.S.E.U.M religious society of Gudja, Malta.

ensuring that the capacity of the Dockyard facilities were fully used and also enhanced the employment in Malta.

These vessels were intended to be rated as gunboats, but were re-rated as sloops (small ships with one mast) in 1884. The dimensions were 167 feet x 32 feet x 14 feet. The machinery for the ship was built at the Malta Dockyard and a special slipway was constructed for the ship still known today as 'Melita Slip'.

During the First World War, the huge losses sustained by the Royal Navy by enemy U-boats, took the vessel from subsidiary service to vessels of the Royal Navy. The ship's name was changed to HMS *Ringdove*. The ship's duties during the First World War are not indicated in the Navy List, presumably for security reasons.[6]

5.7   The Emergence of Trade Unionism

The Dockyard workers demonstrated a unity of purpose in the face of no formal machinery existing through which public servants, individually or collectively, could give vent to their grievances. During the war, a strike was organized at the dockyard in 1917 and the union involved managed to secure a 50% increase in wages instead of the 10% offered by the Admiralty.[7]

---

6   *HM Dockyard, Malta*, W.A Griffiths, 1917.

7   *The Maltese Public Service 1800–1940: The Administrative Politics of a Micro-State*, Godfrey A. Pirotta, 1996.

CHAPTER 6

HMS *Louvain*

6.1 World War One (Naval War)

Compared with the Second World War (with the Battle of the
Atlantic, the Russian and Mediterranean convoys, the major
invasions, and great sea and air battles that raged across the
Pacific), the war of 1914–18 is mainly remembered for the struggle
on land. For most, it conjures up images of trench warfare at Ypres,
the Battle of the Somme, Verdun, perhaps the Eastern Front.

The occasional sea battle (mainly Jutland) appearing out of the
mists together with the U-boat scares towards the end of the war
were the main naval warfare. In fact the Great War at Sea, even
aside from the impact of the British blockade on Germany, was
crucial both to Allied survival and later victory.

If the German High Seas Fleet had defeated the British Grand
Fleet or even broken out into the Atlantic and beyond, Allied
supply lines would have been cut. This did not happen, but the
U-boat warfare of 1917 nearly succeeded.

Aside from the 1914 trade war by German surface ships and
the battles of Coronel and Falklands that followed, together with
the later unrestricted U-boat warfare on the oceans and in the
Mediterranean, most of the naval actions of the First World War
took place in the narrow and inland seas surrounding Europe –
the North Sea and English Channel, the Baltic, the Adriatic and
Aegean, and the Black Sea. In these areas, various "fleets in being"
caused many head-aches to their opponents.

Only one major battle at sea may have been fought – Jutland –
but the navies of the world found themselves in many actions, both

large and small, over the four years, in which good seamen and ships of all nationalities were lost.[1]

6.2   Feeder Lines

There were three main railway companies operating feeder lines during the 19th Century. The fleets of vessels were run by railway companies and were split into different areas as follows:

1. Eastern & North Western companies including Zeeland and Stena Lines.
2. Western & Southern Companies including French and Stena Lines.
3. Scottish & Irish Companies including Stena Lines.

Over the years mergers and takeovers took place as well as the nationalisation of the major companies into the British Transport Commission.

The *Dresden* was a vessel owned by the Great Eastern Railway Company that commenced passenger services to Europe in 1864 from Harwich to Rotterdam and Antwerp, later Hamburg. In 1893 they commenced Harwich – Hook of Holland services and became part of the London & North Eastern Railway Company in 1923. The funnel of the company's vessels between 1864–1923 was buff, black top.

The *Dresden* was of 1,805 tons gross, 302 feet one inch long with a 17 foot 3 inch beam. Five boilers, single ended produced steam at 160 lb./in square to two three cylinder triple expansion engines which drove the twin screws at a maximum speed of 18 knots. Berths were provided for the passengers of these ships mainly situated on the main deck, through the cabin Deluxe were on the upper deck along with the dining room and ladies lounge. Accommodation was described as luxurious.

The *Dresden* was launched at Earls Shipyard, at Hull on 17 November 1896 and it was mainly used on the Harwich-Antwerp route though in June 1897 a few months after entering service represented the Company at the Naval Review at Spithead. On 31 October 1914, the *Dresden* was requisitioned and a small number of the Great Eastern Railway Company crew remained with the ship, mainly engine room personnel, and eventually converted to an armed boarding steamer with two 12-pound guns. It was at this stage that the vessel was renamed *Louvain*.

During the First World War the following other vessels also owned by the Great Eastern Railway Company were either captured or sunk:

Vessel	Built	Service Record (First World War)
Brussels	1902	In 1916 a German warship captured it.
		The Captain was executed by firing squad by the Germans for attempting to ram a U-Boat, which had attacked the ship.
Colchester	1889	It was captured by German warships in 1916.
Copenhagen	1907	It was torpedoed and sunk in the North Sea in 1917

Another vessel, the *Munich* built in 1908 became a hospital ship between 1914–1918 and renamed *St Denis*.

HMS *Louvain* leaving Grand Harbour for the last time before meeting its tragic end

Allied and Neutral Ships lost between 1914–1918 are given in the Table below

	1914	1915	1916	1917	1918
Lost to submarines	3	396	964	2,439	1,035
Lost to surface craft	55	23	32	64	3
Lost to mines	42	97	161	170	27
Lost to aircraft	0	0	0	3	1

6.3   World War One U-boats

During the First World War, the German Imperial Navy utilised different types of U-boats for different purposes such as gasoline-powered boats, Mittel U, U-Cruisers and Merchant U-boats, UB coastal torpedo attack boats, UC coastal minelayers and UE ocean minelayers.

Initially, the German U-boat campaign initiated on 4 February 1915, allowed for the crew to disembark before the vessel was sunk. The deck gun was used in order to conserve the torpedoes. An exception to this rule was the sinking of the Cunard passenger liner, *Lusitania* on 7 May 1915.

In 1916 the German military authorities loosened its sinking policy of giving warnings and all commanders of U-boats were to be fired as long as they did not bear the markings of a passenger ship. Again, in mid 1916, U-boat commanders were ordered not to sink without prior warning, amid threats by America to cut off diplomatic relations with Germany. For a third time Germany changed its policy and declared 'Unrestricted Submarine Warfare' on 3 February 1917, defining *a war zone as an area in which all merchants entering without permission would be torpedoed on sight without warning and without the provision of safety measures for crews and passengers, in the process causing America to declare war on Germany on 6 April 1917.*[2]

President Woodrow Wilson of the United States of America in a speech on 1 February 1917 spoke on this policy:

"….The new policy has swept every restriction aside. Vessels of every kind, whatever their flag, their character, their cargo, their destination, their errand have been ruthlessly sent to the bottom without warning and without thought

---

2   See also *Submarines and Targets: Suggestions for New Codified Rules of Submarine Warfare',* Georgetown Law Journal, Jane Gilliland 1985.

**of help or mercy for those on board the vessels of friendly
neutrals along with those of belligerents. Even hospital ships
and ships carrying relief to the sorely bereaved and stricken
people of Belgium, though the latter were provided with
safe conduct through the prescribed areas by the German
government itself and were distinguished by unmistakable
marks of identity, have been sunk with the same reckless
lack of compassion or of principle…".**

The year 1918 was a year, so far as the British land forces
are concerned, of desperate resistance followed quickly by
overwhelming victory; but for the Navies it was less eventful. The
German fleet, except for its destroyers and smaller vessels, had
sailed for the last time on a hostile errand. The submarines had
been met by the convoys, and British and neutral merchantmen
faced a gradually lessening risk. The year was full of incident, but
free from crisis, until the days when one after the other the navies
of the Central Powers gave up the fight.

The monthly figures of British merchant shipping losses from
all cases had fallen from their high point (169 ships) in April, 1917
to 85 ships in December. The total number of British merchant
vessels lost in 1917 was 1,200; and more than three quarters of
these were sunk by submarines. The total for 1918, to the date of
the Armistice with Germany, was 544 ships (or nearly two million
tons); the highest figure for any month was 82, in March, and the
figures fell to 51 in June and below 50 for each of the following
months. The last two vessels to be sunk by submarines were
torpedoed near Port Said on the 2 November.

Enemy submarines sailing from the East Adriatic ports infested
the main waters of the Mediterranean making them only second
to the English Channel as an operation area for submarine warfare.
These submarines menaced all allied forces that were dependent on
the Mediterranean supply route: in Macedonia, at Salonika, Egypt,

Palestine and those operating against Turkey from the Eastern islands, like Mudros, and at Gallipoli. During the last six months of 1916, U-Boats in the Mediterranean sank 256 ships totaling 662,131 tons. Several U-Boat commanders had great success. Kurt Harting of *U 32* celebrated the New Year, 1917, and his arrival in the Mediterranean by sending three torpedoes into the British battleship *Cornwallis* a few miles off Malta.

During the latter half of 1915, Germany had 15 submarines in the Mediterranean, mainly in the Aegean Sea, where they were positioned against Allied forces in the Dardannelles, and in the Adriatic. This concentration of submarines and the sinking of British battleships, HMS *Triumph* and HMS *Majestic* suggested the use of a small airship to scout for submarines from Malta. However the Admiralty considered seaplanes as a better proposition.[3] (See also Chapter on Aviation History) Otto Hersing of *U 21*, who sank the battleships *Majestic* and *Triumph* off Gallipoli and sank the old French cruiser *Admiral Charnier*, had another success when he sank the liner *City of London* off Malta.

Other ships were victims of submarine-laid mines. The old battleship *Russell* sank after running into a minefield laid by *U 73* in the approaches to Malta. A tragic victim was the 7,308-ton hospital ship *Rewa* that left Malta with 279 patients on board and was torpedoed by Wilhelm Werner of *U 55* despite the fact that the *Rewa* was clearly marked as a hospital ship.

Defences were initially meagre due to a shortage of material. At one time, Malta was defended by a line of painted oil drums to mislead U-Boat commanders into assuming that they were net defence buoys marking the edge of minefields. As allied defences strengthened and the convoy system was enforced, U-Boat

3   *Military Aviation in Malta G.C. 1915–1993*, A comprehensive history, John F. Hamlin, 1994.

successes declined although they remained the main danger to allied shipping until the very end of the war.

6.4   The Sinking of HMS *Louvain*

HMS *Louvain* was sunk with the greatest loss of Maltese lives in one single action during this war (26 Maltese crew and 46 other Maltese ratings were killed on 20 January 1918 in the Aegean Sea) when it was attacked by *UC 22* which was a coastal minelayer type.

John Ellul was a Marine engineer and was employed at the HM Dockyard, in the Fitting shop during 1913 and afloat on repairs of main engines, auxiliary machinery, boiler mounting, both on ships and torpedo boat destroyers. He was also occasionally employed on the various machines in the machine shop and attended steam trials of main engines underway. During the Great War, John Ellul was assistant engineer on HMS *Louvain*. His name is found together with other Maltese crew and ratings totaling 70 who lost their lives. The loss was too great for my grandmother, Josephine Dimech, (nee' Ellul) when she received news of her brother's ultimate sacrifice. She would go out on the house parapet and looking down the hill, would imagine him returning up the hill back home. During this war, Josephine also lost her husband, Armando after having contracted the deadly *Spanish Flu* which was a pandemic that cost the lives of millions of civilians and servicemen alike especially during 1917 and 1918 (See also Chapter 13).

After John Ellul's death the family received a Bronze Plaque, Service medals, booklets showing the Plymouth War Memorial and the names of other servicemen who lost their lives during 1918 as well as a Scroll.

During his service on HMS *Louvain*, John Ellul sent several postcards to his family. The sequence that follows sheds some light on the travels of John Ellul on the HMS *Louvain* and also

Plaque sent "In Memory'" to the next-of-kin. Each had the name engraved on it.

**Assistant engineer
John Ellul**

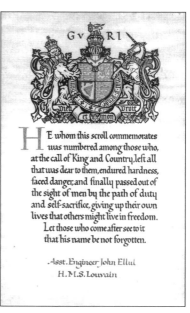

H E whom this scroll commemorates was numbered among those who, at the call of King and Country, left all that was dear to them, endured hardness, faced danger, and finally passed out of the sight of men by the path of duty and self-sacrifice, giving up their own lives that others might live in freedom. Let those who come after see to it that his name be not forgotten.

Asst. Engineer John Ellul
H.M.S. Louvain

Scroll

the contacts he maintained with his family before he died in 1918. Correspondence sent whilst on active duty was carefully scrutinized and censored by the Naval Authorities.

Writing from Alexandria where he was stationed in 1915, he gave news to his mother, Ethelburga Ellul of his sea voyage to Egypt, describing the Egyptian folk and their dress as very colourful saying that most people wore white and green and red, giving he impression it was a Carnival scene. The postcard depicts a wandering (mobile) kitchen with three Egyptian men dressed in traditional dress standing beside it. Alexandria was an important port of call for the Royal Navy with British land bases being maintained to guard the Suez Canal. Britain had full and free use of the harbour of Alexandria. In the event of war or the imminent threat of it, the Egyptian Government gave Britain its full support and unrestricted use of all Egyptian facilities and territory. During the 1914–1918 War, Alexandria also became a great Anglo-French camp and hospital centre, and in 1915 was made the base of the Mediterranean Expeditionary Force.

A post card dated 11 August 1915 sent from Bombay, India was addressed to his brother in law, Armando Dimech who lived in the same house as John Ellul at 51, Marsamxetto Road. John informed Armando that his ship would be leaving Bombay in a week's time en route to Mamargoa, which is near Bombay. He also explained that he shared his cabin with the third Engineer of the ship. He ended his note by saluting the entire household including my mother and my aunt who at the time were toddlers aged 3 and 2 respectively. He also found space on the cover of the card to ask whether my mother had forgotten about him!

Another card dated 16 November 1915 arrived from Bologna. John said that he was at Vastilza at the Corinth Canal. This card bears the stamp 'passed by Censor'. John had arrived from Patras (Greece)and asked his father, Pietro Paolo Ellul to take good care of his Certificates, which he had left behind in Malta. On the front cover of the card he found some space to assert that: *"N.B. I got this p.c. from the 2nd Eng: don't think that I could get one when I like"*.

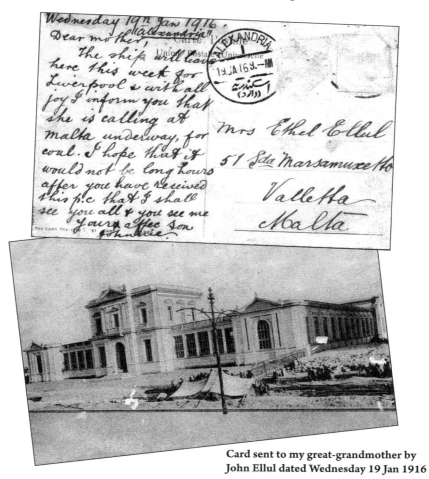

Card sent to my great-grandmother by John Ellul dated Wednesday 19 Jan 1916

The last two cards that I managed to find are dated 19 January 1916, and 11 June 1916. In the first, John wrote to his mother saying that his ship would leave Alexandria that same week en route for Liverpool and with all joy informed her that the ship would call at Malta underway for coal.

The last card described the rough sea after 7 hours of journey since the ship left Malta en route to Alexandria and he said that the ship would be stopping at Alexandria for a fortnight and would call again at Malta on her way back home, but he was not sure of this, as the Captain of the ship had not yet received any orders.

The only means of contact between Maltese servicemen and their families and friends during their duty overseas was through some letter or colourful postcard. The correspondence served to brighten and uplift the spirit of both the serviceman and moreover his family who knew very well what kind of perils is to be found at sea and on land. There were occasions when the ships passed through Malta and the Maltese crew and ratings were given leave to meet their families as witnessed in the cards sent by my relative John Ellul.

Mail not arriving to Malta or arriving very late was also very frequent and due to the illiteracy rate, (not many could read or write), there was, a risk in trusting someone to write a card or letter on one's behalf with the words being misunderstood or even

MEMORIALS TO THE NAVAL RANKS AND RATINGS OF THE EMPIRE WHO FELL IN THE GREAT WAR AND HAVE NO OTHER GRAVE THAN THE SEA

The Register of the names inscribed on the Memorial at the Port of Plymouth

PART SIX   1918—21

Compiled and Published by order of the Imperial War Graves Commission, London.   1924.

"**Front cover of Memorial Book** sent to relatives of the men who have no other grave than the sea!"

worst still misinterpreted, causing much anguish or even family trouble.[4]

A colourful collection of French, Italian and English cards bearing handwritten well wishes in the Maltese language were kindly made available by Mr Raymond Cachia, whose grandfather, Anthony and his grandfather's brother L. Cachia served in the First World War.

Anthony Cachia served in the Royal Army Service Corps in France, Italy and Ireland during the Great War and during service overseas, sent many postcards to his wife Gaetana assuring her of his health and safety. L. Cachia brother of Anthony served on the **HMS** *Valiant* and he also sent postcards to his family.

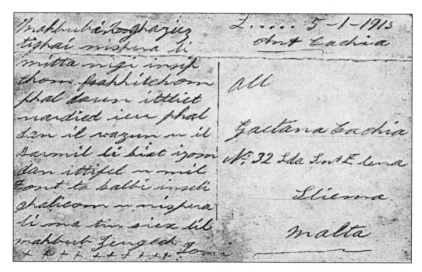

(By courtesy of Mr Raymond Cachia)

---

4   For further information on Postal Services during the Great War, see *Gallipoli: The Malta Connection*, by John Anthony Mizzi, p169, 1991. Mr Mizzi quotes Malta – The Postal History & Postage Stamps, Malta Study Circle (Robson Lowe, 1980). An interesting exposition is given on Malta's postal history and as to how the Allies made efforts to expedite mail to and from Malta in spite of the war and the increased submarine warfare in 1917.

One particular card is addressed to Mrs Cachia at her address No. 32 Strada Sant Elena, Sliema, Malta and is dated 5 January 1915 whilst another is dated 17 September 1918.

6.5   UC 22

The *UC 22* was built at Blohn & Voss Shipyard in Hamburg and launched on 1 February 1916 was under the command of Carl Bunte between 1 January 1918 and 16 May 1918, and the ship's total successes during the war were 24 ships sunk (warships excluded) totaling over 52,000 tons.

The first contingent of German submarines surrendered at Harwich on the 20 November 1918; and on the following day the High Seas Fleet arrived at Rosyth on its way to internment at Scapa Flow, where their own crews scuttled the battleships and cruisers on the 21 June 1919.

A group of Engine Room Artificers from British submarines relaxes in the Maltese sunshine during 1915. Harold Lindsay Smith is second from left Artificer-Engineer H. Lindsay Smith, R.N., son of Mrs Smith, of 90, Coventry Road, Market Harborough, has been awarded the D.S.C. for distinguished service with the submarines. By 1918 Harold Lindsay Smith was serving on the L10. Sadly, on 4th. October of that year the vessel was lost with all hands, believed to have been rammed, the only L Class submarine to be lost in the war. Harold had served in submarines since 31st July 1914, when the Royal Navy was mobilised and had survived in this most hazardous service only to lose his life just a few weeks before the war's end.[5]

---

5   *http://www.harboro.ndirect.co.uk/malta.htm*

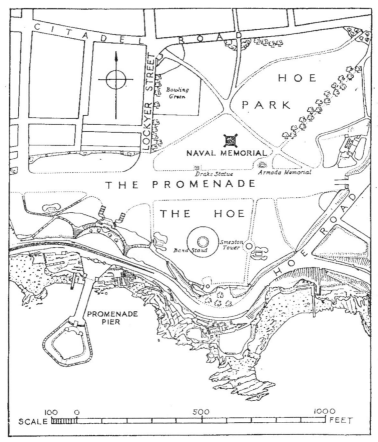

PLAN OF PART OF THE TOWN OF PLYMOUTH

Above: Site of Plymouth memorial
Left: UC 29

CHAPTER 7

HOSPITAL FACILITIES

7.1 Casualties of the Great War

Despite intensive research by historians, there is no – and there will never be – a definitive list of the casualties (totals of those killed or wounded) inflicted during World War One. Where detailed record-keeping was attempted the demands of battle undermined it, as the destructive nature of the war, a conflict where soldiers could be wholly obliterated or instantly buried, destroyed both the records themselves and the memories of those who knew the fates of their comrades.

Casualities of the First World War

Country	Mobilised	Killed	Wounded	Total
Africa	55,000	10,000	unknown	unknown
Australia	330,000	59,000	152,000	211,000
Austria-Hungary	6,500,000	1,200,000	3,620,000	4,820,000
Belgium	207,000	13,000	44,000	57,000
Bulgaria	400,000	101,000	153,000	254,000
Canada	620,000	67,000	173,000	241,000
The Caribbean	21,000	1,000	3,000	4,000
French Empire	7,500,000	1,385,000	4,266,000	5,561,000
Germany	11,000,000	1,718,000	4,234,000	5,952,000
Great Britain*	5,397,000	703,000*	1,663,000	2,367,000
Greece	230,000	5,000	21,000	26,000
India	1,500,000	43,000	65,000	108,000
Italy	5,500,000	60,000	947,000	1,407,000
Japan	800,000	250	1,000	1,250

Country	Mobilised	Killed	Wounded	Total
Montenegro	50,000	3,000	10,000	13,000
New Zealand	110,000	18,000	55,000	73,000
Portugal	100,000	7,000	15,000	22,000
Romania	750,000	200,000	120,000	320,000
Russia	12,000,000	1,700,000	4,950,000	6,650,000
Serbia	707,000	128,000	133,000	261,000
South Africa	149,000	7,000	12,000	19,000
Turkey	1,600,000	336,000	400,000	736,000
USA	4,272,500	117,000	204,000	321,000

Source: Casualties of the First World War, Robert Wilde, 2003
*Included in this figure are 592 Maltese Servicemen as per Malta Government Gazette of 19 November 1938.

The War not only produced its own categories of infectious diseases such as the *Spanish Flu*, that was spread at seaports and accounted for more lost lives than those killed on the battlefield, but also casualties suffering from psychological and psychiatric conditions caused by the combat stress. The breakdown in behaviour associated with shell shock was not clearly recognised. 332 British soldiers were executed in the war suffering from shell shock and a campaign is still running to get these men officially forgiven (but was not recognised by military, then, as a genuine reason for failing in your duty). As a matter of fact there are few reports of causalities that might be considered of a psychological nature during the initial period of the war.

Situated at the crossroads of the Mediterranean, Malta's strategic position for welcoming the sick and injured of the many bloody campaigns of the Great War was positively exploited by the British authorities by furnishing it with a high bed-strength and top-rate medical consultants and surgical specialists.

The contribution of the Maltese medical profession during the war was highlighted in a speech by the Acting President of Malta,

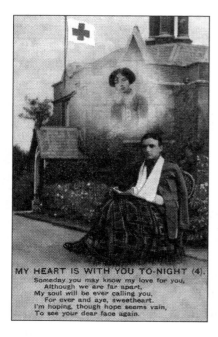

MY HEART IS WITH YOU TO-NIGHT (4).
Someday you may know my love for you,
   Although we are far apart,
My soul will be ever calling you,
   For ever and aye, sweetheart.
I'm hoping, though hope seems vain,
To see your dear face again.

**A typical card sent by the wounded to
their loved ones**
(Courtesy of Raymond Cachia)

Dr George Hyzler.[1] Dr Hyzler made reference to Dr Peter Paul Debono (later, Prof. of Surgery at the Royal University of Malta), who, soon after having qualified, proceeded to England for Post Graduate Studies. At West London Hospital he followed a course in anaesthesia. There he became familiar with the administration of ether, nitrous oxide and spinal anaesthesia. On his return to Malta during the First World War he used this experience at the British Naval Hospital at Bighi where he was an anaesthetist. Here he began using spinal anaesthesia. Later on he introduced it into civil practice.

Writing in the *Sunday Times of 1 December, 2002,* in the feature titled '*Nurse of the Mediterranean*', *Major Maurice Micallef-Eynaud* comments that once Egypt could not cope with the influx of

1   Speech delivered by the Acting President of Malta, Dr George Hyzler during the Annual European Congress of Regional Anaesthesia held at the Mediterranean Conference Centre, Valletta on 10 September 2003. Department of Information.

Gallipoli campaign casualties, the buck was passed to Malta with the evacuation of 500 venereal diseases cases to the island. Malta was the only alternative in the Mediterranean as Cyprus was too close for comfort, Greece was neutral and Gibraltar was too far away and much too small.

The build-up of Malta's medical services is succinctly described in the above feature. Lieutenant-General Sir Alfred Keogh, the top medical officer at the War Office, ordered a rapid expansion of Malta's medical services and authorised immediate and large-scale purchase of beds and medical equipment.

7.2   Transport of casualties

Since the dawn of history humans have been engaging in conflicts and so much has been written on the campaigns of war but little has been recorded concerning the wounded and their transportation, care and treatment. There are different methods of transporting the wounded:

- By men
- By contrivances carried by men or wheeled by men
- By contrivances wheeled by men
- By animals
- By contrivances carried by animals,
- By mechanical means (charabancs, cars, trains, aeroplanes and helicopters)
- By water transport (barges steamers and hospital ships)

Many of the wounded of the First World War arrived in Malta by Hospital ships. Three categories of ships were used for this purpose: the Hospital ship, Hospital carrier and Ambulance transport.[2]

---

2   In all 2,550 officers and 55,406 other ranks passed through some 28 military hospitals and other centres in Malta during the Gallipoli campaign. The majority of those who succumbed to their injuries or sickness are buried at Pietà.

A hospital ship was a vessel fitted for the transport of sick and wound to take 500 beds and the staff included medical and surgical specialists and nursing sisters. A *hospital carrier* was a passenger steamer temporarily adapted for the conveyance of sick and wounded during the period when hospital ships were being fitted out. Both the above ships were protected by international conventions and therefore were neither available nor would be used for the transport of armed personnel or war material. They flew the Red Cross flag and the hulls were usually painted white with a green band and one or more Red Cross emblems on each side.

An ambulance transport was a vessel which, used on the outward voyage for the transport of troops, was fitted for the homeward voyage either partly or wholly to carry sick and wounded. It had no distinguishing marks and could claim no protection under the international conventions. The medical equipment of an ambulance transport could be as complete as that of a hospital ship. It was used, therefore, for the less serious cases of sickness and wounds and was not used at all if accommodation in hospital ships could be made available.

The motor ambulances came to Malta during the First World War. Before that time patients were conveyed to hospital in a primitive and most uncomfortable manner. The well to do were carried in a 'caleche' or, later, in a cab, sometimes even a spring cart, but the paupers were always taken to hospital on a litter constructed like a stretcher on wheels '*katalett tar-roti*'.[3]

7.3   Hospital Ships

The Gallipoli campaign brought to Malta, Mudros, Alexandria and Imbros a large number of ships carrying wounded from the

---

3   *Melita Historica*. Vol. 4 No.4, pp. 278–280, 1967. 'Before the motor Ambulances came to Malta', by Professor Joseph Galea.

battlefront. The transport included hospital ships, troop ships and other vessels. In August-October 1915 alone, more than 50,000 casualties were transported to Malta, Gibraltar and hospitals in the U.K. The following list shows the risks of hospital ships ferrying wounded to Malta due to the 'unrestricted submarine warfare' and mines of the German Imperial Navy:

HMHS *Souden*	arrived in Malta in 1915
HMHS *Franconia*	torpedoed and sunk in 1915
HMHS *Dover Castle*	torpedoed in 1917
HMHS *Goorkha*	mined in 1917 off Malta. There were 362 survivors including 17 nursing sisters. The ship was then towed into Grand Harbour.

As in the Crimean War period, the presence in Malta of so many casualties ferried from the battlefronts of the First World War reduced Malta to a hospital and convalescent centre, which increased the risk of contagious diseases. The Hospitalier role of Malta was revived during this war with over 27 hospitals providing 25,000 beds being set up.

From Spring 1915, hospitals and convalescent depots established on the Islands of Malta and Gozo dealt with over 135,000 sick and wounded servicemen, arriving mainly from the campaigns in Gallipoli and Salonika The increased submarine attacks on transport ships as a result of the unrestricted submarine warfare (resumed by the German Navy in February 1917) reduced the flow of hospital ships to and from Malta as from May 1917.

A hospital ship at Grand Harbour with the floating dock in the background
Between 1915 and 1919 there were 494 visits by hospital ships

7.4   The Red Cross and St John's Ambulance Work

Formed in 1099, the Order of St John was formed of religious knights who all trained in medical care. They were the first to bring the concept of medical care in the battlefield to armies in Europe. The concept of laypersons providing pre-medical care arose from wars of the 18th and 19th century. In 1863 the First International Geneva Convention was held, and John Furley represented the Order to St John in the creation of The Red Cross, the purpose of which was to provide '*aid to sick and wounded soldiers in the field*'. The Red Cross emblem is a reversal of the Swiss flag to represent the Host Country of the Geneva Conventions, and the white cross of the Swiss Flag is actually a version of the banner of St John.

In 1877, the St John ambulance was formed '*to train men and women for the benefit of sick and wounded*'. The association focused on training ambulance crews for railways and mines, as well as ambulance police. The term FIRST AID first appeared in

1878, created by executives of the St John Ambulance Association as a blending of the terms 'first treatment' and 'National Aid'. In 1880, the word First Aid was popularised with the publication of a textbook '*First Aid to the Injured*'.

At first, only doctors could teach first aid, and another doctor would test students. During World War One, an explosion of civilian involvement in first aid in Commonwealth Countries (including Malta) was experienced, and it was even taught to most school-children.[4]

The St John's Ambulance Brigade, Malta was set up in 1909

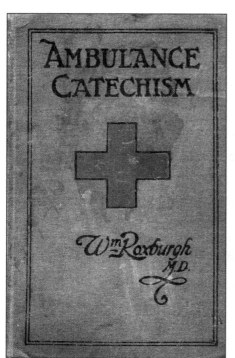

with the main object being to train and maintain a body of men and women thoroughly efficient in First Aid and Auxiliary Nursing. The Brigade developed these objects to meet the changing necessities of time. The Brigade has a Cadet Code of Chivalry with the prime aim to serve God and Mankind. The Brigade is organised in different sections, divisions, and a Corps consisting of sections and divisions. There is also The District part of the

Cover of a First Aid Book used in military hospitals during the First World War

<hr />

4   See, *St John Ambulance Halton Hills serving North Halton, a Brief History of First Aid* www.sja-haltonhills.org, 16 January 2004.

Brigade's organisation, which refers to all Brigade Units in Malta and Gozo.

With the outbreak of the great European War in 1914, the Knights of St John in the British Empire put all their resources on a scale that had never before been imagined. The nature of their work was varied and their beneficent influence was exercised through many different channels. Their work fell into three main classes:

- The provision of personnel to supplement the medical reserves of the Naval and Military forces of the Crown.
- The Hospital at Etaples and other Hospitals dependent upon the Order.
- The work of its Committees and Departments at St John's Gate.

On 10 August 1914, an appeal for funds was made to the public and the War Office ordered that the Order's ambulance Department was to form part of the Red Cross organisation of Great Britain, and was recognised by the British government under the terms of the Geneva Convention as a Society to assist the Medical Services in time of War.

To reach this goal in October 1914, a Joint War Committee of the two Societies was formed for the purpose of dealing with the Government, for the delegation of work, appeals for funds, and the publication of financial and other reports.

The Joint War Committee was very active in the East and Sir Courtauld Thomson was appointed Chief Commissioner for Malta, Egypt and the Near East. Great depots of ambulance stores were established at Malta, Alexandria and Salonika, from which at one time 75 hospitals, 50 hospital ships and 5 hospital trains were being supplied, and during the Gallipoli operations the Committee was maintaining 10 hospitals in the Near East. By the beginning of 1917 as many as 110,000 men and women were working in detachments of the Red Cross, the Order of St John and the Territorial Force Associations.

The work that was done by the Order during the war, is perhaps best exemplified by the direct relief that was given to the sick and wounded in the Order's hospitals; most of these was the Hospital at Etaples, which was considered as one of the best of its type in France.[5]

Intensive training courses for the Brigade were undertaken in many districts of Malta and Gozo. Over 40 surgeons and 100 ambulance Members were attached to Naval and Military Hospitals. Several Surgeons performed duty on Italian Hospital Ships that were evacuating British sick and wounded to England.

The *Malta Government Gazette of 10 August 1917* listed the following Members of the Brigade with citations indicating "*specially valuable service rendered to the Empire during the present war.*":

Major H.A Balbi, District Superintendent

Lieut. Colonel R.P. Sammut, Corps Surgeon

Capt. W.R. Gatt, Corps Secretary

Capt. A.J. Gatt, Corps Treasurer,

Dr A.V. Bernard, Divisional surgeon and Corps Secretary (Dr Bernard also received through the Secretary of State for the Colonies, the special thanks of the Army Council.)

Dr S. Ellul Grech and Dr A. Marras, Surgeons

Mrs A.G. Mifsud, Superintendent of the Nursing Division

Mr C. Tagliaferro, Corps Superintendent of Stores

---

5   The work of the Order during wartime is given in the official history of the British Order of the Hospital of St John of Jerusalem in, *The Knights of St John in the British Empire*, by Colonel E.J. King, St John's gate London, 1934.

In September 1914, a detachment was formed and offered their services in France: 4 surgeons, 3 divisional officers, 6 nursing sisters, and 34 other ranks volunteered but the offer was not accepted, as it was considered that their services would be more useful in Malta.

Over 40 Surgeons and 100 Ambulance Members were attached to Naval and Military Hospitals. Several surgeons performed duty on Italian Hospital Ships that were evacuating British wounded and sick to England. 10 Members of the Nursing Divisions were enrolled as VAD's for fulltime work and 20 more performed part-time service. Members who were unable to undertake nursing duties rendered assistance by visiting hospitals, meeting hospital ships and distributing refreshments and other comforts to the patients and working in the Comfort Depots.

In 1915, a detachment of the Brigade composed of 9 Ambulance Members under Surgeon A. Marras M.D., preceded to Mudros for duty with the Maltese Labour Corps. Other Ambulance Members

PUBLIC HEALTH DEPARTMENT.

NOTICE.

Owing to the exceptionally heavy rains of the 22nd instant, it is inadvisable to use, for at least fifteen days, any water for drinking purposes unless it has been boiled.

A. CRITIEN,

A/ Chief Government Medical Officer
and Superintendent of Public Health.

23rd November, 1915.

performed duty with Maltese Units in Macedonia and other war zones.

The arrival in Malta of large numbers of sick and wounded during the Gallipoli campaign stressed the resources of the St John's Ambulance Brigade to their limits and a call for supplementary staff of the Services became very urgent in 1915. Several Base Hospitals were established in Malta.

7.5   Hospitals

Malta's hospitals served the just cause of healing and attending to the sick and dying serviceman indicative of the sheer hard work inputted by the Maltese and British nursing organisations.

7.5.1   Valletta Military Hospital

The role of this hospital was that of a sorting depot of the sick and wounded arriving at the Maltese principal port of Valletta on hospital ships. After being visited by the doctors they were transferred to the other 30 hospitals and camps scattered over the Islands. The Hospital itself was also reserved for dangerously ill cases that could not be safely moved. The increase in the flow of wounded servicemen necessitated an augmentation of the number of beds from 26 to 340. A renovation of disused wards was made, bringing the medical facilities in line with the sanitary and medical standards of the time.

7.5.2   Zammit Clapp Hospital in St Julian's

(also known as Blue Sisters Hospital)

This was run by the Little Company of Mary and commenced as a Seamen's Hospital as from 29 August, 1911. This hospital was originally opened in the limits of St Julian's at the beginning of the 20th Century. The hospital played an important role during the First World War caring for the sick and the injured. The Sisters provided the nursing and other services associated with hospitalisation, whilst the government supplied the surgical appliances, bedding, clothing and drugs.

The Seamen's Hospital was transferred to the King George V Memorial Hospital in 1922 when it was inaugurated in the same year. This hospital was built as a memorial to the men of the Merchant Navy who died in the First World War.

7.5.3   Mtarfa Hospital

Towards the end of the 19th Century a small 50-bed hospital was build at St David's Barracks at Mtarfa. This served to treat the soldiers' families, the troops continuing to receive treatment at the Cottonera Hospital. The services related to maternity were administered and staffed by the Royal Army Medical Corps

Plans to augment this hospital were initiated in 1912, and the new Mtarfa Hospital was opened in June 1920. The hospital after the Second World War was disbanded and re-formed under the name of David Bruce Military Hospital

7.5.4   Spinola Palace

In St Julian's another hospital that had been closed down in 1860 was re-opened at Spinola Palace to cater for the increasing number of wounded. During the First World War the Royal Army Medical Corps (RAMC) had requisitioned it.[6]

The RAMC had the following main duties:

1. The maintenance of health and the prevention of disease. An Army Manual of Hygiene and Sanitation was the standard book for this purpose.
2. The care and treatment of the sick and wounded
3. The collection and evacuation of the sick and wounded in the field
4. The preparation of professional records of the sick and wounded

By late 1915, 334 RAMC doctors had been deployed in Malta and 2,032 medical orderlies.

During the First World War, Spinola Palace received troops suffering from venereal disease. This hospital was named Forrest Hospital after the principal Medical Officer of the garrison serving during 1860. It was closed down in 1922. Venereal disease was a constant problem with all nationalities of soldiery.[7]

7.5.5 Bighi Hospital

This hospital accommodated a very large number of casualties arriving from the Dardanelles campaign. The characteristics of this hospital were very large corridors shielding the patients from the summer midday sun and from inclement weather. The wards were about 30 ft in height and to each patient were allowed some

---

6   The RAMC was responsible for the immediate treatment of the sick and wounded, their collection and transportation from the fighting areas, their care, treatment and discipline while in medical units or when sick in quarters, the compilation of statistics and records of general and professional interest regarding them, and the replenishment of medical equipment.

7   See, *Military Hospitals in Malta,* C. Savona-Ventura

1800 cubic feet of air. The patients were bedded down in corridors and ditches.[8]

7.5.6   Cottonera Hospital

This was the principal and largest military hospital in Malta in the first year of the war enjoying modern facilities and the best location. It provided 167 beds out of a total of 278 beds available on the Island. This hospital was built in 1837 and considered as one of the best in southern Europe. In 1929 the War Office leased it to house St Edwards college.

This hospital treated of casualty evacuations from the Gallipoli and Salonika campaigns in 1915 and 1916–1917 respectively, and thousands of dysentery, enteric group, trenchfoot, arthritis, malaria and shell-shocked patients. Due to the dreadful and very unsanitary conditions prevailing in both these campaigns, these cases far outnumbered wounded personnel after the initial stages of these two campaigns.

The hospital received 141 surgical cases from the *Goorkha* hospital ship (mentioned in Section 7.3, which hit a mine about 15 miles Northeast of Malta in 1917). Dr Charles J. Boffa mentions this incident and also presents a feature of his late father Dr Lawrence Boffa, titled '*Malta – The Nurse of the Mediterranean*' which appeared in *Malta Today, June, 1970*.[9]

---

8   See also, *Royal Navy Hospitals, Malta*, the sick quarters of His Royal Highness Prince Alfred, The Illustrated London News, April, 1863.

9   *Malta's grand Harbour and its environs in War and Peace*, DrCharles J. Boffa, pp. 40–47, 2000

7.5.7   Fort Chambray Hospital

During the First World War, the Fort (situated in the sister island of Gozo) served as a hospital relieving the crowded camps in Malta. From October 1915 to March 1916, no less than 1,579 men recovering from illness or injuries passed through the fort and were returned to active service. The medical staff at the time issued a record of their experiences in a journal entitled '*The Fort Chambray Gazette*'. The fort closed down as a Convalescent Depot in March 1916.

Casualties from the Gallipoli landings and Salonika Expedition were brought to Fort Chambray in large numbers. October and November 1915 recorded an average of 2,000 men per week from Gallipoli, and during one week, from 2 to 9 December a record 6,341 wounded from Salonika arrived. The numbers fell quickly, so much so that by the end of March 1916, the convalescent Depot was closed down.[10]

7.5.8   Other Hospitals

Other hospitals and hospital camps were set up during the First World War including the following:

- **Hamrun Hospital**. The Bugeja's Institute at Ħamrun was converted into a 100-bed hospital.
- **St Andrew's Hospital.**
- **St George's Hospital.**
- **St Paul's Hospital** (close to St Andrew's).
- **St David's Hospital and St Patrick's Hospital.**
- **St John's School**, Sliema. This became a 510-bed hospital in July, 1915. (*see also below in Requisitioning of schools section*).

---

10   See also *http:website.lineone.net/-remosliema/chambray.htm*

- **St Ignatius Hospital** (in the old Jesuit College in St Julian's). This had been vacated by the Jesuits in 1907 and was equipped as a 155-bed hospital in July, 1915.
- **Tignè Hospital.**
- **St Elmo and Baviere Hospitals in Valletta.** St Elmo School became a 318-bed hospital for surgical cases and the Auberge de Baviere became a 130-bed hospital reserved for very severe surgical cases; mostly cranial and spinal injuries.
- **Manoel Hospital.**
- **Għajn Tuffieħa Camp.**[11]

The enemy's submarine campaign eventually made the crossing of the Mediterranean so dangerous that in April 1917 the Malta hospitals were closed down. By that time no less than 125,050 officers and men had been received and cared for. This could only be achieved as the result of the excellent organisation and of the co-operation of one and all.

Lord Methuen, the governor of Malta wrote,

"I am glad that I came to Malta if it was only to help the country in the organisation of these hospitals...The people in Malta, ladies and gentlemen, came to my aid in a manner I shall never forget".

7.5.9   Requisitioning of Schools

Despite the increase in attendance and numbers of scholars on school registers, in September 1915 only one-fourth of 600 children seeking admission to school were in fact admitted. The shortage of schools was further compounded by the Government's granting of permissions to the Military Authorities in June 1915 to use the Valletta (Strada Mercanti) Schools for sick and wounded

11   *Military Hospitala in Malta*, C. Savona-Ventura

Ghain Tuffieha Camp Hospital   MALTA

St. Paul's Hospital Camp.   MALTA

Convalescent Camp., Ghain Tuffieha   MALTA

Convalescent camps

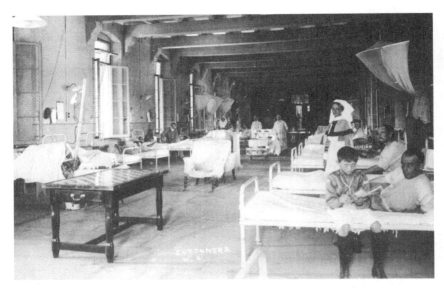

The main ward at Cottonera Hospital with a scout reading a newspaper to one of the patients
(Courtesy of Mr John A. Mizzi)

soldiers, and the Governor sanctioned also the use of Lower St Elmo and the Garrison Infant School (near Auberge de Baviere) for school purposes. These premises afforded all the accommodation required, and schools proceeded without any interruption.

In August 1915, Government granted a similar permission as regards Sliema Schools: St John's Hospital (in the Sliema Primary School) the Elementary Schools were able to carry on as usual, in September, at "the Cloisters", in the "*Juventutis Domus*" and in the Carmelite Monastery, St Julian's", which were generously and free of charge, placed at the disposal of the Elementary Schools' Department by Judge Antonio Micallef, LL.D. The Very Rev. Father O'Grady, S.C., Rector of the Salesians and the Very Rev. Professor A. Cuschieri, O.C. Provincial of the Carmelites.

7.6   Tas-Sliema and First World War Casualties[12]

During the First World War (1914–1918), Malta served its role to the British Empire in three ways: Naval Base, Hospital, and a source of manpower with many Maltese engaged in the Army and the Fleet as well as numerous others recruited in Labour Corps serving overseas in Salonika and Italy. The useful contribution that Malta provided as a huge Hospital facility earned it the name of. "*The Nurse of the Mediterranean*".

In 1915, Britain decided to attack the Dardanelles in Turkey, and for this purpose British and Empire troops were sent to serve in this campaign. The sick and wounded were brought to Malta and later on from Greece, when Britain invaded Salonika (Greece).

In the first few months of the war, which had started in August 1914, there was no indication that Malta could be used as a hospital facility. But, an enquiry about accommodation for the wounded arrived from Egypt during February, 1915 and prompted the preparation of a scheme for the establishment of 3,000 beds for the sick and wounded in Malta and also for convalescent cases in Gozo. The arrival of thousands of wounded in Malta led to the setting up of 27 Hospitals distributed over Malta.[13]

Tas-Sliema's Contribution

Two hospitals were prepared in Sliema, one at Tigné Barracks and the other at the Primary School, which was purposely converted into a hospital and named 'St John's Hospital'. A Tea Room was also opened in Sliema for the wounded. Religious Orders and other

---

12   This feature has been kindly made available by the author, Winston L. Zammit B.A (Hons.), M.A. and has been translated from the Maltese language by Mr Zammit's permission. It appeared for the first time in *Lehen il-Banda Cittadina "Sliema", Festa tal-Madonna tas-Sacro Cuor, 2002,* under the title '*Tas-Sliema u l-Feruti ta' L-Ewwel Gwerra'.*

13   *British Malta*, A.V. Laferla, Vol II, pp. 200–201, Malta 1947.

Tea Room at St Patricks School in Sliema

establishments also lent a helping hand in alleviating the suffering of the sick and wounded.

The first 600 wounded troops arrived in Malta on 4 May 1915. The majority of these were convalescent cases. A local newspaper gave a vivid description of the arrival of these first troops:

> **"At Sliema the passage of the ambulance service conveying the wounded to Tigné created quite a sensation. The inhabitants turning out *en masse* to welcome the heroes. Amidst loud cheers flowers were thrown into the vehicles whilst several of the more ardent admirers approached with chocolates, cakes and cigarettes".[14]**

Eight days later, on 11 May 1915, another contingent of 800 wounded arrived. The Hospital Ship arrived at the Sliema ferries

---

14   *Daily Malta Chronicle*, 6 May 1915.

and the troops were transported to St Andrew's and Pembroke. The description of this event had also been documented as follows:

"The men were transported to the mole well covered and protected from the sun. On arrival they were welcomed by the Ladies of St John's Ambulance Brigade and the British Red Cross Societies, and other ladies who served them from liberally furnished tables erected on the Mole. Enormous crowds gathered in the neighbourhood".[15]

Tigné Hospital

Although the first wounded were taken to Tigné, this hospital was not opened before 14 June 1915. This was to be a General Hospital run by Surgeon Major Robert Randon R.M.A., a Maltese Doctor. The hospital had 676 beds and later the occupancy was increased to 1,100 beds.[16] This hospital was closed on 9 January 1919. During its operation, many sick and wounded died.[17]

Apart from the services offered by the staff of the hospital, the sick and wounded of Tigné were also offered the assistance of some organisations.[18] The women's committee of the British Red Cross Society, distributed books and other articles,[19] whilst the La Vallette Mandolin Society organised a concert.[20] With regard to spiritual needs, Archbishop Dom Mawru Caruana OSB visited

---

15   *Ibid*, 14 May 1915.

16   From notes written by Surgeon Major Robert Randon, who was appointed Medial Officer-in-Charge, Hospital, Tigné, on 17 May 1915. This information was passed on to the author of this article by his son Dr Goffredo Randon LL.D in a letter dated 1 October 1987

17   See *Daily Malta Chronicle* of 12, July 1915, 13 July 1915, 13 July 1915, 22 July 1915, 24 July 1915 and 27 July 1915.

18   Apart from Dr Randon, there were other doctors at this hospital, amongst whom, Dr V. Bonavia who performed the duties of Civil Surgeon. See, *Daily Malta Chronicle* of 9 January 1917.

19   *Daily Malta Chronicle* of 19 May 1915

20   *Ibid.*, 2 June 1915

the hospital on 23 May, 1917 and administered the Sacrament of Confirmation to several soldiers at Tigné, Manoel and Mellieħa and also to some students attending school.[21] To alleviate the sick troops' inconvenience, the Archbishop also ordered a reduction in the frequency of the ringing of church bells around several parts of Malta, including Sliema.[22]

St John's Hospital

In 1915, the Sliema Government Primary School (that had been completed in 1910) was converted into a Hospital. A local newspaper stated:

"The Government Elementary School at Sliema has now been opened as a hospital, with 200 patients under the name of St John's Hospital".[23] The hospital had library facilities, and some activities were organised for the wounded.[24]

Tea Room

Soon after the arrival of the first wounded cases in Sliema, the Union Club Committee put at the disposal of the Women's Committee of the St John's Ambulance Brigade and the British Red Cross, part of their club premises at Għar id-Dud. It was decided that a Tea Room be opened daily during the week between 4pm and 7pm for the wounded servicemen and an appeal was made for the donation of certain items for this aim.[25] This Tea Room was inaugurated on Thursday 20 May 1915 and for the opening a large number of wounded troops attended,[26] so much so that by June between 120 and 130 were present daily. Donations were also not lacking and by

---

21   *La Diocesi*, 7 June, p.309, 1917.

22   *Malta*, 5 June 1915

23   *Daily Malta Chronicle*, 2 September 1915.

24   *Ibid.*, 21 September 1915, 22 January 1916, 25 April 1916.

25   *Ibid.*, 18 May 1915.

26   *Ibid.*, 22 May 1915.

21 May 1915 a sum of £37.5s.4d. had been collected[27] The Kavalier Lancellotti quartet also gave musical representations on Tuesdays and Fridays.[28]

Other Activities

The Military authorities also ensured that the convalescent troops were kept entertained. The Australia Hall at Pembroke, St Andrew's was ready for it's opening in January 1916. The inscription on the facade of the building stills stands in a pitiful and abandoned state reads:

> **'Erected in November by the Australian Branch of the British Red Cross society for the benefit of the soldiers of the British Empire'.**

Another event for the benefit of the recreation and entertainment of the servicemen was the opening ceremony of the New Church Army Soldiers Club was opened on 8 February 1917 at St Julian's by Governor Methuen.[29]

The Government organised several, religious, social, sports and recreational activities in other parts of Sliema, apart from the Tea Room. In January, 1916, 100 convalescent cases from the two other hospitals were invited for tea at the Imperial Hotel,[30] and during February 1917, a number of convalescent cases were invited to watch films at the Conqueror Cinema.[31]

On St Patrick's Day (18 March) of 1917, a Sports Day for the wounded and convalescent Irish troops was held at St Patrick's School. Governor Lord Methuen and Archbishop Dom Mawru

---

27   *Malta*, 9 July 1915.

28   *Daily Malta Chronicle*, 10 June 1915.

29   A detailed description of the inauguration ceremony is found in *the Daily Malta Chronicle* of 9 February 1917.

30   *Ibid.*, 29 January 1916 and 3 November 1916.

31   *Ibid.*, 6 November 1917.

Caruana OSB attended this activity. A large number of events were organised and prizes were distributed. 750 persons were served tea.[32] In 1918, St Patrick's Day was celebrated again in the same school and religious functions, shooting competitions and an athletic meeting were organised and tea was served to 500 convalescents.[33]

The Closing Down of the Hospitals (1919)

The First World War ended on 11 November, 1918. Up to the last week of January, 1919, the majority of the hospitals and Convalescent Camps were either closed or being closed. A local newspaper commented that:

"only a few hundreds of thousands of convalescents remain on the Island and these are likewise being sent home".[34]

Tigné Hospital was closed down on 6 January, 1919. Another Chapter in the history of Sliema and Malta was wound up.[35]

Hospitality shown by Maltese Families

During the First World War, the house where we (Family Zarb-Dimech and Family Zammit-Dimech) live at 7, St Julian's Hill, St Julian's (then, 4, St Julian's Hill, St Julian's) was owned by my great grand father, Pietro Paolo Ellul who, during the war, spent some time, living with his daughter, Josephine and her husband, Armando, at Valletta. Mr Ellul had acquired the house at St Julian's by way of donation from his parents Gugliermo and Marianna Ellul on 29 January 1888 and he used it as his residence as from November 1916.[36]

---

32 *Ibid.* 4 April 1917.

33 *Ibid.*, 27 March, 1918.

34 *Ibid.*, 27 January 1919.

35 Notes by Major Dr Robert Randon, op. cit

36 From family records.

Towards the end of April 1915, the military authorities in Malta were unprepared for the great influx of wounded servicemen arriving in Malta and many a Maltese affluent family offered their chauffeur – driven motor car to take wounded servicemen to hospitals.

As soon as the wounded were released from hospitals as convalescent cases, many Maltese families welcomed them in numbers varying from 8 to 10 at their homes, inviting them for tea and manifested to them utmost care and affection, (a true characteristic of Maltese Christian hospitality). Those wounded that could not be invited at Maltese homes were often taken around Malta by many Maltese and shown around the most interesting places and historical monuments.[37]

About 40 years ago, an elderly English lady by the name of Ms. Margaret Utting used to visit our house at St Julian's and recounted that convalescent servicemen were welcomed to the house as guests. This was not only a gesture of friendship but also an act of Christian charity to speed up the recovery of the servicemen. This story told by my cousin, John Zammit-Dimech has also been corroborated by my mother in that she remembers of a certain Mrs Burrows who leased the house from Mr Ellul.

---

37   *Il-Gbira Guerra tad-Dinja, Vol. I*, Opra Colossali li tigbor fiha l-ahjar fattijet tal guerra mehuda minn fuk cotba ta potenzi nuetrali Propieta' Letteraria u Artistica ta Andolfo & Magro, Stamperija u Legatorija ta' Emilio Lombardi, 28, Strada Santa Maria, u 27, 28, Strada San Trofimo Sliema. pp. 276–279, 1920.

Chapter 8

The Gozitan Casualties

Note: See Appendix D for list of Gozitan Casualties
(Translated by kind permission of Mr Charles Bezzina).[1]

The Maltese Islands were not directly involved in the First World War, as was the case in the Second World War. During the Second World War Malta and Gozo suffered much to the extent that the population was on the brink of starvation. The Islands withstood the brunt of aerial bombardments, which wrought havoc on the people causing much sacrifice. The First World War was to prove a different story.

Malta as a 'Nurse'

Malta served as a Mediterranean Nurse to the British servicemen arriving in Malta, mostly during the Dardanelles campaign, around April 1915. Dr Herbert Ganado in his masterpiece *Rajt Malta Tinbidel* presents this account on the arrival of the sick and wounded in the Maltese harbour.

"On 4 May 1915, the first wounded arrived in our country. The hospital ships, painted white with large red crosses of the Red Cross on their sides, entered Grand Harbour in an air of grief and sorrow. The morbid spectacle brought memories to some old folk looking from the balconies on the side of the Baracca. They remembered and recounted the scene some 60 years before when the sick and wounded started arriving from the Crimean War.

---

1   Mr Charles Bezzina of Victoria Gozo has kindly made available the list of Gozitan casualties at Appendix D. Mr Bezzina is a historian and poet who published several books on the history of wartime Gozo and poetical works. This painstaking research by Mr Charles Bezzina involved a lot of work and the list appeared for the first time in the Maltese language in the Magazine *l-Għid ta' l-Assunta, Gozo, 2002.*

As soon as word spread that the casualties from Dardanelles were entering the harbour, the Baracca and the bastions were filled with people. There was no band playing, as was the case when the French fleet arrived. There was, so to say, an eerie silence that is usually found around the bed of someone who is gravely sick in hospital.

Strada Rjali was full of people, but in the middle of the road there were no people. The Police were re-routing traffic for this sad occasion. The silence on the part of crowd pressing on opposite pavements gave the semblance of a Good Friday Procession. Many held cigarette boxes, others held bags filled with chocolates purchased from Blackley and the Opera bar...

Around Malta, albeit not from the start, some 27 hospitals were completed, with a bed-capacity of 20,000. At *Għajn Tuffieħa* there were camps to accommodate 4,000 convalescent cases. There were some 300 British and Maltese doctors. And some 1,000 nurses arrived from England. There were countless Maltese employed at military hospitals. And some of the most qualified and competent doctors arrived from England such as Balance and Garrot...

By the end of May, some 4,000 casualties arrived in 8 hospitals and by September 10,000 had arrived. Up to March 1916, hospital-beds reached a capacity of 20,000. In all, Malta welcomed some 80,000 casualties ...

On 25 September, 1915, some time before all the troops had disembarked from Gallipoli, the British and French landed in Salonika to aid the Serbian army who was pressed severely by the Germans, Austrians and Bulgarians..."

(note: Translated from Maltese)

8.1   Gozitan Casualties

It is not my intention to describe the bloody battles of World War One. The Somme, Dardanelles, Ypres, and Verdun are names associated with campaigns that cost the lives of thousands of soldiers from both sides.

I am now in a position to give a good indication of the Gozitan victims of the First World War and this, after an extensive research. The Gozitans who died served as soldiers in Salonika, seamen on Warships in the Battle of Jutland (at the end of May 1916) and in other circumstances, such as those who died at Air and Naval Bases or at Taranto harbour, in Italy.

During the last period of the war, around September 1916, about 800 Maltese and Gozitans volunteered to serve in the Labour Corps to help the British in their battle against German and Bulgarian troops in Salonika, Greece. Subsequently, other Maltese battalions kept arriving, to the extent that there was quite an appreciable number of Maltese and Gozitans in Salonika.

Two Employment Companies left Malta (the first in February and the other in September 1918). During this period, the Allied Forces faced an undulating task in the liberation of Serbia against the Central Powers, particularly Bulgaria, In September 1918 a huge offensive, was launched by the Allies forcing the Bulgarians to agree to an Armistice at the battle of Monastir.

During the years 1916–1918, about 100 persons, that formed part of the Maltese Labour Corps lost their lives as a result of enemy action, illness and other circumstances. This figure includes several Gozitans, who were employed or engaged in this Corps and who gave their contribution, until they were killed in action.

In the detailed list presented here, I have included not only the Gozitans who joined the Malta Labour Corps, but also many others who died on Merchant Ships or Naval Warships as well as others who died in other circumstances. Apart from the interesting information, about the Gozitan victims that was presented by Dun Dumink Camilleri in his book, '*Mitt Jien Biex Tgħix Int*', some other information, such as the sinking of ships and the rest, is being published for the first time.

I followed suit in the footsteps of my late father, Frank Bezzina (1925–1996) who went into great efforts, so that the names of the war dead of 1939–1945 are immortalised in publications. In the process, the memory of the Gozitan dead is kept alive. Our labours have been crowned with this presentation of the Gozitan war dead for the 1914–1918 war. This list should act as a spur to Local Councils to commemorate these victims as they truly deserve in their hometown or village.

During the years 1915–1918, the Salonika front witnessed an outbreak of malaria in which thousands of allied soldiers were taken sick. Around 481,000 were hospitalised of which 18,000 were war casualties. The Salonika campaign remains controversial. Despite achieving victory over Bulgaria, and holding the progress of the Central Powers, the price in human lives was exaggerated for the Allies.

It is interesting to note that the Gozitan artist, Tommasu Zahra (*Majsi ta' l-Ghadmu*), son of Guzepp and Karmena nee' Vella, (well known for the Christmas Crib figures (pasturi) and other clay figures he used to make), was recruited in the Malta Labour Corps with other Gozitans. Majsi was unmarried together with his brother and two sisters (Toni, Guditta and Filomena). He lived at Triq San Ġorġ. On 11 February 1917, he was about 30 years old and wrote to his brother from Salonika:

Dear Brother,

I am well, thank God as I hope you are well too. I am very happy because the work is not so tough in the Camp. I am with *Toni ta' Saver tal-Mewta* and *Ġanni il-Bajdi* and many other Gozitans.

I send you my best wishes and regards and to the barber and all my friends as well as *Barabba* and *Brejbex*. Dear brother tell *Ċikku tal-Cortis* that when I arrive, I will finish it for him.

Bye
Tommaso Zahra
11.12.1917

Note: Translated from Maltese

Majsi Zahra (tal-Għadma) in the middle together with Cikku l-Bajdi and Toni tal-Mewta: three Gozitan soldiers at Salonika

CHAPTER 9

PRISONERS OF WAR

9.1   Standing Orders

During the First World War enemy prisoners were assessed and internment camps were established. Very few records of individual internees survive for the First World War in the National Archives of the Home Office of the United Kingdom. Prisoners of war in Malta were mainly held at **Verdala Barracks, St Clement Camp and adjacent camps (Żejtun), Salvatore Fort and Polverista Barracks** until March 1920 and men of the Royal Malta Artillery guarded these. By the middle of 1916 there were no less than 1,670 prisoners from Austria, Germany, Bulgaria, Turkey and Greece. The Officers and men of the King's Own Malta Regiment of Militia guarded the prisoners of war.

The international agreements on the treatment of prisoners sprang from the founding of the Red Cross in Geneva in 1863. The first agreement, established in 1864 and eventually accepted by 48 states, dealt briefly with the 'Amelioration of he Wounded'. The second, concluded in 1906, extended protection to the sick and wounded, to those treating them, and to the treatment of wounded and sick prisoners of war. Twenty-three years later (ten years after the end of World War One), a third convention was signed that included a separate section covering the rights and treatment of prisoners of war.[1]

In 1918, the Governor of Malta and Commander in Chief approved for information and guidance, Standing Orders for the Prisoners of War, Camp, Malta. The Commandant's Office of

---

1   *Hitler's Third Reich*, Volume 10 p. 17

the Prisoners of War Camp, Lieutenant-Colonel Neale in turn published these standing orders on 1 February 1918.

The Prisoners of War were by Article 8 of the Annex to the Hague Convention, 1907, *"subject to the laws, regulations, and orders in force in the Army of the state in the power of which they are."* These laws, etc., which were contained in the Army Act and various books of regulations which govern the English Army were enforced in order that prisoners of war comply with all rules and regulations deemed necessary for their safety, good order and discipline.

The standing orders covered general and special orders as follows:

1. General Orders

These orders covered every aspect of life in the camps from rules whereby prisoners of war would be fired upon, improper or derogatory language, salute, mustering, damage to property (rooms tents etc,), cleaning, bedding, election of mess President or Captain, permission to send letters and other formalities on writing letters, newspapers and receipt of parcels, smoking, possession of personal property, lighting of camp, hospital visits, and the drawing of money.

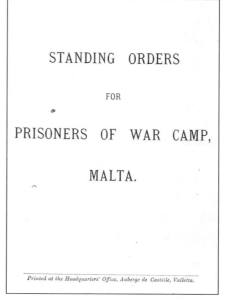

STANDING ORDERS

FOR

PRISONERS OF WAR CAMP,

MALTA.

Printed at the Headquarters' Office, Auberge de Castille, Valletta.

Cover page of booklet on Standing Orders for P.O.W. Camps

2. **Special Orders**
- Regulations to be observed in Special Messes
- Instructions for the Permanent Fatigue Party in Verdala Barracks
- Abstract of the regulations relating to the treatment and conduct of prisoners of war undergoing close confinement
- Undeliverable parcels for prisoners of war
- Powers of attorney

Captain (then Major, later ADC to the Governor) William Raphael Gatt was appointed as Commandant, Prisoners of War Camp by the War Office on 19 May 1920.

At first the atmosphere in the camps was relaxed but the successful escape from Verdala and Malta by Ensign, Fikentscher and an Austrian civilian internee in 1916 led to more restrictions and a more vigilant guard. All privileges were denied and for the next two years the prisoners were not allowed out of Verdala despite the lack of exercise space for a camp population of 400. Until the entry of the United States into the war, the United States Consul in Valletta officially represented the prisoners. Afterwards the Swiss Consul looked after their interests.

Captain William Raphael Gatt, Commandant P.O.W. Camp

```
C.R.Malta 37396                War Office
                          LONDON S.W.1
041/1523 M.S.1.A.            19th May 1920

Sir,

    Inreply to your letter No 37396(M.S.) dated the 9
1st April 1920 relative to Captain W.R.Gatt, I am dir
ted to inform you that approval is given to his appoi
ment as Commandant, Prisoners of War Camp, and to be
temporary Major whilst so employed, with Command Pay
of six shillings per day.


                    I am

                       Sir,

        Your Obedient Servant,
                         Staff
            (sd) H.H.Stacke.Capt
                        for Lieut.General

                    Military Secretary

The Field Marshal
    Governor and C-inC
       Malta.
```

Captain Gatt's appointment as Commandant

The hundreds of prisoners of war and civilian internees hailed from all nations allied to the Kaiser's Germany and these included Egyptians, Arabs and Greeks, suspected of being German sympathisers. The following are some of the most 'illustrious' prisoners of war.

9.2 The captain crew of the German cruiser 'Emdem'

This warship under the command of captain von Muller was sunk after a successful commerce-raiding cruise in the Indian Ocean. The Captain and the ship's officers – including Lieutenant Franz Josef, (Prince) Von Hohenzollern of the German Royal Family (nephew of the then King of Romania) – were locked up in the Verdala Fort whilst the crew were interned in a nearby Fort.

In 1915, the prisoners set up The German-Austro-Hungarian aid organisation, later being joined by the Turks. Von Muller was president of this organisation set up to help those prisoners, which were bereft of any resources. In 1917 von Muller was transferred to Britain but the rest remained in Malta until the end of hostilities.[2]

9.3   Karl Doenitz

Amongst the most famous German prisoners to be held captive in Malta was Karl Doenitz, who in the Second World War (April 1945) was overseeing the last major operation conducted by Hitler's navy: the evacuation of over 2 million civilians and soldiers from the Eastern Front. Karl Doenitz was Grossadmiral, Commander-in-Chief of the Kriegsmarine under Hitler's command. *Doenitz* was also the architect of the Nazi German submarine campaign during the Second World War.

Karl Doenitz

On the outbreak of the First World War, Doenitz was serving abroad the light cruiser *Breslau*. Doenitz asked to be transferred to the expanding submarine fleet, showing the verve and courage of a youth ambitious in his career. He joined *U 39* in January 1917. He sailed on 5 war patrols Germany as the German Imperial Naval resumed 'Unrestricted Submarine Warfare' on 1 February 1917. This was a policy of indiscriminately attacking Allied and suspicious natural shipping, both military and merchant with submarine torpedoes.

---

2   Information about von Muller kindly made available by Mr Louis Henwood.

Doenitz's first command was a small minelayer *UC 25* in March 1918. His next command was *UB 68* but disaster stuck on 4 October 1918 as he attempted to attack a convoy in the Mediterranean. The escorts were wide-awake and the sloop *Snapdragon* blasted the submarine with her guns to such effect that Donitz had to scuttle his boat and surrender. He and most of his crew were taken prisoner. He spent the rest of the War in Malta and later in Britain.

9.4   Liman Von Sanders

General Liman Von Sanders was in command of the Turkish Army on the southern front in Syria until he was defeated by Field-Marshall Allenby in 1918, when he handed over the command to Kemal and returned to Constantinople. There he surrendered to the Allies, and was interned in Malta until the summer of 1919.

Von Sanders was the head of the German Military Mission sent to Turkey by Germany in 1914 and the author of many changes in the Turkish Army. German officers, technicians and instructors began to appear at first in scores and then in hundreds taking over the control of the munitions factory in Constantinople and many guns along the Bosphorus and the Dardanelles.

Von Sanders was a calm and steady man and was an inspired choice for implementing these changes. He was a man genuinely absorbed in the technique and tactics of strategy and with all the impressive authority and intelligence. The army was his life and was not distracted by politics.

9.5   Turkish Prisoners of War

For the first months of the war, there had been much religious persecution by the Turks, and the Armenians in Turkey were the scapegoats in receiving an organised and brutal hatred against them resulting in massacres and slaughter. The extermination process was fuelled on many grounds that the Turks tried to justify for their cruelty.

According to British Foreign Office Dossiers on Turkish War Criminals, a collection of British documents on various perpetrators and agents of the Armenian Genocide who were rounded up by the British and interned on Malta pending trial were published by Vartkes Yeghiayan.

Liman Von Sanders

Unfortunately the internees were given to Mustafa Kemal's Nationalist Government in order to secure the release of British officers and soldiers held by the Nationalists. There also exist microfilm copies of the British records on the Malta internments.[3]

9.6   Geo Furst

Born in Nuremberg in 1888, Furst was in Malta as secretary to Baron Max Von Tucker, the German consul who built Villa Luginsland on the Buskett road. The Baron had married Victoria Maempel who was the previous Consul's daughter, while the architect of villa Luginsland was Francesco Zammit whose descendants are the Zammit Maempels. The German consul left Malta before the outbreak of hostilities, as diplomats had the facility to leave to avoid being interned.

Furst married another architect's daughter, Helen Debono, however this did not prevent him from being interned at Verdala

3   This information has been sourced from
http://www.armeniangenocideposters.org/html/foreign

during World War One and repatriated in World War Two. Furst produced several books about Malta that are illustrated by his wonderful photographs.[4]

9.7   Rudolf Hess in Malta?

In the *Malta at War Journal Vol No p28*, sources were quoted, showing that Rudolf Hess was held prisoner of war in Malta during the First World War. The feature also carried images of a postcard sent by Rudolf Hess to his family dated 17 May 1915. Reference was also made to the *Times of Malta* of 7 December 1941 wherein Major Edward John Briffa de Piro recalled that he had been adjutant to the prisoners-of-war camp at Verdala Barracks when Hess was president of one of the many messes in which the camp was divided.[5]

The claims that Rudolf Hess's was interned in Malta are very questionable in that according to the *Institute for Historical Review* (IHR), Rudolf Hess's son, Wolf Rudger Hess in a videotape presentation at the Eleventh IHR Conference of 1992 gives the front line combat service of his father. Nowhere does it result from his son's presentation that Rudolf Hess was ever a Prisoner of War, let alone in Malta, during the period covered by the documentation and sources provided by Malta at War.

'...The start of the First World War in 1914 found the family at its vacation home in Bavaria. Rudolf Hess, then 20 years of age, did not hesitate for a moment before reporting as a volunteer with the Bavarian Field Artillery. A short time later, he was transferred to the infantry, and by November 4, 1914, he was serving as a poorly trained recruit at the

4   *Times of Malta (Weekender)*, 31 January, 2004 pp10–11. Book review by Kenneth Zammit Tabona on Giovanni Bonello's book, *Histories of Malta*

5   *Malta at War*, Volume I, Page 28, by John A. Mizzi and Mark Anthony Vella, 2001

front, where he took part in the trench warfare of the first battle of the Somme.

Along with most young Germans of that time, Rudolf Hess went to the front as a fervent patriot acutely conscious of Germany's cause, which he regarded as entirely just, and determined to defeat the British-French arch enemy. After six months of front-line service, my father was promoted to lance corporal. To his men he was an exemplary comrade, always the first to volunteer for raids and reconnaissance patrols. In bloody battles among the barbed wire trenches and shell craters, he distinguished himself by his cheerful composure, courage and bravery.

By 1917 he had been promoted to the rank of Lieutenant. But he also paid the price of this "career" advancement. He was gravely wounded in 1916, and again in 1917 when a rifle bullet pierced his left lung.

Scarred by the hardships and wounds of front line duty, on December 12, 1918 – that is, after Compiegne – Rudolf Hess was "discharged from active military service to Reicholdsgrun without maintenance," as the official army record rather badly puts it. This is, without pay, pension or disability allowance.

Already during the war, the family had lost its considerable holdings in Egypt as a result of the British expropriation...'.[6]

During the Second World War Rudolf Hess was Hitler's deputy. He is famous for his flight to Scotland on 10 May 1941 where he parachuted to negotiate a peace with Britain. He was tried after the Second World War at Nuremberg and sentenced as a prisoner

---

6   See, *Journal for Historical Review* feature, A Son's Struggle for His Father's Honor, The Life and Death of My father, Rudolf Hess.

of war in the Allied Military Prison in Berlin – Spandau until his death 1987 aged 93. Given this research, it would be more plausible to say that it was Rudolf Hess's father (Adolf) who was intermed in Malta.[7]

9.8   Internees Mail

Internees kept contact with family and friends by means of letters and cards that were censored by the British military authorities. Such mail may be found by sifting through stamp and mail auctions that are held by *JB Stamp Auctions*. An interesting list of auctions (Number 38) is being presented as an illustration of internees' mail:

A card received by a German P.O.W. at Verdala
(Courtesy of Sliema Stamp Shop)

---

7   Information kindly provided by Mr Stephen Petroni.

- 1915 (21 June) Postcard from Niederdorf to the Verdala Barracks, Cospicua, Malta, addressed to Hans Gungenhauser, Prisoner of War at this camp. The postcard shows the Niederdorf postmark flanked with the "**POST FREE PRISONERS OF WAR**".
- 1916 (February) Cover sent by G. Hurzar Prisoner of War at Verdala Barracks to an addressee in Zurich. The cover was sent "free from the Prisoner of war" camp.
- 1916 (30 July) Postcard sent free by Prisoner of War, Wilhelm Rustemeyer from Verdala Barracks to Germany.[8]

---

8   See *JB Stamp Auctions*, Auction Number 38, p23, Sliema Stamp Shop, 91, M. Dimech Street, Sliema

Opposite and above: Celebrations at the Verdala Camp were not lacking as this 1915–1916 programme reveals.
(Courtesy of Mr Andrew Cauchi)

A caricature of St Clement Camp, Żejtun Post Office. This drawing appeared in a newsletter of January, 1916. The newsletter was printed and distributed by the German P.O.W.'s.
(Courtesy of Mr Andrew Cauchi)

The cover page of the newsletter drawn up by German P.O.W.'s
(Courtesy of Mr Andrew Cauchi)

CHAPTER 10

WAR GRAVES AND MEMORIALS

10.1 Commonwealth War Graves Commission

War cemeteries rarely fail to move visitors, many of whom express their surprise and sorrow to find that there are often so many cemeteries in a small area, which is particularly true of the First World War battlefield areas.

The Commonwealth War Graves Commission's work was 'completed' during the 1930s. There were burials and commemorations in over 100 countries, ranging from the largest cemeteries with tens of thousands of graves, to isolated, single-grave sites. The degree of care, which goes into maintaining them all is immediately apparent and is often, remarked upon in the visitors' books.

The care of British and Commonwealth war graves and memorials from the two World Wars is entrusted to the Commonwealth War Graves Commissions. (Originally, the Imperial War Graves Commission)

The Commonwealth War Graves Commission is responsible for the marking and upkeep of all British war graves. Most graves are in the commission's cemeteries, but not all of them are. Some of the fallen were buried in cemeteries such as Communal Cemeteries. Many other British and Empire serviceman and woman who lost his or her life in either of the two world wars and who have the sea as their final resting place are commemorated by name by inclusion on one of the Memorials to the Missing.

In many countries, the national governments gave the land, on which cemeteries or memorials stand, to Great Britain, or the Commonwealth Countries, which had a significant number of burials at a given site.

The work of the Commission goes on, even so long after the Great War. Even now, from time to time, the body of a 'missing' British or Commonwealth serviceman may be found. Whenever, this happens, the Commission makes every effort to find and inform the next-of-kin. There will then be an appropriately solemn burial of the remains in a military cemetery and the serviceman 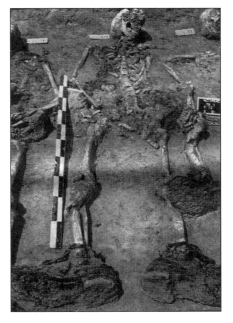 will have his own grave and headstone. Following this, his name will be removed from whichever Memorial to the Missing previously contained it.[1]

Comrades in arms even in death

---

1   *The Daily Mail of Thursday, June 21, 2001*, Article by Anne de Courcy titled "Comrades in Arms – Even in Death", gives a detailed account of 20 soldiers of the Lincolnshire Regiment, a unit known as Grimsby Chums whose remains where unearthed from a mass grave after 84 years in Arras, Northern France. After this discovery, these men were buried with fully military honours in an official war grave.

10.2 Naval Cemetery Rinella

This Cemetery once belonged to the Admiralty and is now under the responsibility of the Commonwealth Graves Commission. There are 477 First World War graves at this cemetery.

On examining the cemetery reports and cemetery plans, joint and collective burials of Commonwealth servicemen from both wars took place During the Second World War Graves had to be hewn out of the rock and this was very dangerous due to the threat of air raids.

During the Great War a Japanese Naval contingent was stationed in Malta and the most tragic story of their assignment in Malta was when 67 crew members of the Japanese destroyer *Sakaki* were killed when the *U 27* (an Austro-Hungarian) submarine torpedoed the ship on 11 June 1917. The dead were buried in Malta and now lie in peace at the Kalkara Military Cemetery.[2]

The Japanese Navy had come to the Mediterranean to protect British naval vessels from German U-boats. In a feature, in the *Times (Malta)* of Saturday, 27 March 2004, titled 'Japanese lieutenant's son visits war dead at Kalkara cemetery', 68 year old Yutaka Sasaki, son of Chikashi Sasaki, (who had come to Malta in April 1917) explained in an interview that at that time his father was the lieutenant and chief engineer of the newly built destroyer *Matsu* of the Japanese Royal Navy. He was 26.

In a book Chikashi Sasaki wrote in 1955 (in Japanese) and which was published in Japan, entitled *'Experience the Grace of God'*, he describes how on June 11, 1917, the Destroyer *Sakaki* had been hit and how on the following day, he had been ordered to collect dead bodies, and fuel to burn the dead whose remains had been buried at Kalkara where the Monument of the Japanese royal Navy was later built. Mr Sasaki has many albums full of photographs taken

---

2   *The Naval War in the Mediterranean*, 1914–1918, Paul G. Halpern, 1987

by his father during his experience in Malta. Mr Sasaki said that in his book, his father also wrote about attending services at St Andrew's Scots Presbyterian church in Valletta.

The Japanese Navy had saved 2,500 men (crew and soldiers) who had been on the British ship *Transylvania*. The ship had sunk but the men were saved and the Japanese soldiers had been thanked by Britain for their deed. Mr Sasaki's father had also been given the George Cross Medal by the British Parliament shortly after leaving Malta.

In 1921, Hirohito the Emperor Shouwa, (1901–1989) arrived in Malta for a 3 day stop on his way to Gibraltar. The Emperor arrived on Sunday 24 April, 1921. The following day, he visited the Cemetery where he laid wreaths at the memorial to the Japanese Sailors. Within this cemetery is also a Memorial for German Prisoners-of-War of World War One. A Memorial was also placed over the graves of the Maltese servicemen who lost their lives in the explosion at HM Dockyard in 1915 described in Chapters 5 and of this book.

The Cemetery is divided into two sections, Protestant and Roman Catholic. There are 351 Commonwealth burials of the Great War (5 of which are unidentified) found in the Protestant section, the rest are found in various other areas elsewhere. There is also standing in the Protestant section a granite Cross of Sacrifice which was erected after that war Among those buried

The memorial to the Japanese sailors who lost their lives in defence of the Mediterranean during World War One

in the cemetery are 44 men from HMS *Egmont*, the Depot ship at Malta and 22 who died when HMS *Russel* was sunk by a mine off Malta in April 1916.[3]

10.3 Imtarfa Military Cemetery

There are over 10 First World War and over 200 Second World War casualties commemorated in this site. The burials include service personnel and members of the Foreign Office (civilians) attached to the Prime Minister's delegation for the Yalta conference, who were killed in a flying accident on the way to the Crimea. The War Graves Commission maintains this cemetery.

10.4 Pembroke Military Cemetery

This cemetery is situated just off the north-east coastal road that runs from Msida through St Andrews and to St Paul's Bay, between St Andrews and what was formerly St Patrick's Barracks.

Ta Braxia Cemetery (Circa 1901)

3   See also Reports and Plans of the Capuccini Naval Cemetery, Rinella, Malta

This cemetery was begun in 1908 by the military authorities to serve the garrison. There are 9 Commonwealth burials of the First World War and 315 burials of the Second World War. There are also 269 non-world war burials. Within the cemetery lies the Pembroke Memorial which commemorates 52 servicemen of the 1939–45 War whose graves in other parts of Malta are so situated that permanent maintenance cannot be assured. Their names appear on marble plaques let into the plinth of the Cross of Sacrifice.

10.5 Ta' Braxia (Pietà) International Cemetery

The Cemetery is located on the edge of the Gwardamanga district; the entrance is on Triq Il-Principessa Melita, leading to Triq Tal-Pietà and Msida Sea Front and Creek. Pietà was the principal garrison cemetery and is the largest resting place for First World War casualties. It is laid out in rectangular paved terraces.

Ta Braxia Cemetery

This Cemetery is close to *Portes des Bombes* and was opened in 1857 replacing a small group of cemeteries on the bastions in Floriana, which were virtually full. Emanuele Luigi Galizia who was later responsible for the much larger Addolarata cemetery designed it. The Cemetery is open to all religions for the purpose of burial.

Here are over 1,000, 1914–1918-war casualties commemorated in this site. Of the 1914–1918 graves, 5 were brought after the Armistice from the *Lazaretto Cemetery*, 2 from outside *Addolorata Cemetery* and 1 from the *Gozo Cemetery*. There is also a tablet erected commemorating 13 Indian soldiers and 7 men of the Indian Labour Corps, whose bodies were cremated at Lazaretto Cemetery at Manoel Island during World War One.

Cemetery records show that from World War One, there are the graves of:

- 989 United Kingdom Soldiers
- 170 Australian Soldiers
- 61 New Zealand Soldiers
- 25 Men of the Royal Navy
- 10 Royal Marines
- 8 Men of the Royal Air Force
- 7 Men of the Indian Army
- 3 Men of the West Indian and British West Indian Regiments
- 2 Women of the Queen Alexandria's Imperial Military Nursing Service, and one each from Territorial Force Nursing Service, Canadian Medical Unit, Royal Newfoundland Regiment, King's Own Malta Regiment, Merchant Navy, Serbian Relief Fund, and Russian Labour Corps.

It is noted that a known grave of a holder of the Victoria Cross is found at this Cemetery. This is of Captain Andrew Moynihan of the Cameroonians (Scottish Rifles) who died in the Crimean War on 8 September 1857.

10.6 Addolorata Cemetery, Paola

The Santa Maria Addolorata Cemetery was designed by Emanuele Luigi Galizia, (1830 – 1906), of the Public Works Department, and opened on 9th May 1869. Several thousand burials have taken place since then, as it is the main Roman Catholic cemetery in Malta, the faith followed by almost 100% of the population. It is predominantly for civilians, but servicemen and their families have used it during peacetime, as well as during World War I and World War II.

10.7 The Turkish Cemetery

Before the recent cemetery, there was another one known as *Tat-Torok*. This was already built before 1675 and it was used to bury Turkish slaves that died here. This was changed into a piece of land upon which the current cemetery was built. The local Government gave the land. In 11th June 1873, Antonio Nahum Duharcy who was the Ottoman Sultan's Consul and the Hon. Dr Giovanni Battista Trapani, Collector of Territorial Revenue went to the notary F.S. Camilleri, where they signed the contract in which the local Government gave the land known as *Ta Sammut* so that a new cemetery could be built there and instead the Turkish Consul gave the old cemetery. The cemetery was built from the money of the Turkish Government for the burial of the Muslims. Architect E.L.Galizia built it in 1874 using a Muslim architectonic style and design. When it was completed the remains from the old cemetery were taken to the new cemetery. In March 1928, when the Knight F.K. Gollcher was the General Consul of Turkey, there were 103 unidentified Muslims buried there, 24 that had died in an accident on board the ship *Sardegna*, 6 French, 6 English, and 23 Turkish prisoners of war that died in Malta. Two inscriptions, one in Turkish and another in French say: *Meta x-xemx titgħawweg, u l-kwiekeb jibdew jaqgħu, mill-oqbra mħattmin mill-mewt, iqumu mqallbin, u minn din is-sodda ta' trab. imqajmin mir-raqda, joħorġu kollha dija, ulied tad-din u tat-talba.*

10.8 War Memorials

10.8.1 War Memorials (Britain)

The Memorial at the Port of Plymouth (Index Number Memorial Register 2, Part Six 1918–21) is one of many memorials to the naval ranks and ratings of the Empire who fell in the Great War and have no other grave than the sea. The Register records the names of those Officers and Men of the Navies and the memorial is found on the North side of Plymouth Hoe (see also chapter 6). The names of those who fell in the other years of the war are recorded in other Registers. Other Memorials are also found at Chatham and Portsmouth.

The Register of the Plymouth Memorial records particulars of the loss of 1,198 ranks and ratings of the Royal Navy, 275 of whom fell in HMS 'Louvain', 'Bittern' and 'Anchusa', 20 sailors of the Royal Australian Navy, 1 of the Royal Australian Naval Reserve, and 1 of the South African Royal Naval Volunteer Reserve, 1 member of the Women's Royal Naval Service and 8 civilians employed by the Admiralty.

The particulars given in the register of the names have been compiled from information furnished by the Admiralty and the next-of-kin. In all cases the relatives were asked to furnish the personal information they wished to appear in the Register and where possible this had been given in their actual words.

The names on the Memorials are arranged alphabetically by ranks and ratings under the year of death, on a series of bronze panels, which are numbered. The number which concludes each entry in the Register is that of the panel on which the name appears.

This Register is the most dramatic for the Maltese and Gozitan families who lost one of their beloved. The Register contains the names of 46 ratings and 24 crew members of the HMS *Louvain* and also other Maltese seamen who perished in the last year of the war. The sinking of the HMS *Louvain* meant the loss of the greatest number of Maltese servicemen in one single war action.

10.8.2 War Memorials (Gallipoli)

There are over 30 Commonwealth cemeteries, 1, French and 24 mostly symbolic Turkish cemeteries. The bones of those buried hastily on death still lie scattered over the area and these frequently surface after the rains or else washed ashore on the beaches of Gallipoli in this grim reminder. The British and Empire casualties have been calculated at 470,000, besides 47,000 French.

There are over 60 memorials; that at Helles are overlooking the entrance to the Dardanelles, contains panels with the names of ships sunk and regiments engaged in the fighting and nearly 4,400 names of those whose bodies were never found; The Chanuk Bair Memorial commemorates 825 officers and men of the New Zealand Expeditionary Force, who died in that sector of the fighting and the LonePine memorial carries the names of 3,268 missing Australians and 252 buried at sea (as well as 252 New Zealanders who were never found or were buried at sea) and here are also 1,167 graves.[4]

4   *The Sunday Times (Malta)* 28 January, 2001, Book Reviews on the Gallipoli campaign by John Anthony Mizzi. p. 32

The Helles Memorial at the south-western tip of the Gallipoli Peninsula commemorates 20,763 United Kingdom (including Maltese), Australian and Indian servicemen.[5]

10.8.3 War Memorials (Australia)

The Australian War Memorial at Canberra where the name of Charles E. Bonavia, B Coy, 11th Bn, 3rd Infantry Brigade, 1st Australian division is remembered. His name also appears on the Lone Pine Memorial at Gallipoli.

10.8.4 War Memorial (Floriana)

On 11 November, 1938 – 20 years after the signing of the Armistice, which ended the First World War, Malta a new National War Memorial was unveiled at an Armistice Day ceremony at Floriana as a special homage to the nearly 600 Maltese (numbered with the nearly million men of the British Armed Forces) who died in the war.

War Memorial (Floriana)

The War Memorial was built to the design of Louis Naudi of the Malta Museum. On the memorial were inscribed the names of 592 Maltese who had been killed in the First World War. After the Second World War, four tablets reproducing Malta's

5   *Gallipoli: The Malta Connection*, John Anthony Mizzi, 1991

Armorial bearings, King George V's message, King George V's letter awarding the George Cross to Malta in 1942 and President Roosevelt's citation of the following year replaced the names on the monument.

10.8.5 King George V Merchant Seamen's Memorial Hospital

This was built in memory of the merchant seamen who perished in the 1914–1918 War and rebuilt after its destruction in the second World War. This Hospital is now known as Boffa Hospital.

10.8.6 King's Own Malta Regiment Memorial and Royal Malta Artillery Memorial

The President of Malta, Dr Vincent Tabone, unveiled the Royal Malta Artillery Memorial on 3 April, 1991 and the King's Own Malta Regiment Memorial on 14 February, 1993.

10.8.7 Gozo War Memorial

Gozo has no War Memorial for the Gozitan victims of the First World War. A War Memorial was unveiled on 7 May 1954 by Her Majesty Queen Elizabeth II during her one-and-a half hour visit to Gozo. This consists of a nine-foot bronze statue of Christ the King placed on a pedestal, 12 feet high, cut from hard *Qala* stone.

Gozo offered to Christ the King the sacrifice of its Beloved Fallen during the Second World War and Christ in return blesses this Sacrifice. The Sacrifice is symbolized by a Cross stretching along the front part of the pedestal beneath whose arms are inscribed the name of the fallen. The four bas-reliefs are: Army – a soldier is nursing a wounded comrade; Navy – a sailor on a warship; RAF a pilot standing near his machine; Civilians – a woman with a child in her hand weeping over her dying husband

The names inscribed on this monument does not include all the Second World War Gozitan victims and as shown in Chapter 8, the monument includes some names of Gozitan Victims of the First World War which were entered by mistake.

The author shares the same sentiment as many Gozitans that a First World War monument for Gozitan victims is erected. Way back in 1954 a committee was set up for this purpose to study various projects presented by local artists. The design chosen for the Second World War monument was that of Mr Paolo Pace of Victoria, who at that time resided in Rome.

A new monument would not only be a fitting tribute for the First World War Gozitan victims but would also correct the mistakes entered in the present monument for the Second World War Gozitan victims.

CHAPTER 11

SOCIAL ADMINISTRATION

Note: See Appendix E: List of Relief Funds

11.1 Education

The absence of free and compulsory education in Malta meant that Government provided few facilities and this was especially so at the secondary level and for the education of girls. It was only the rich who could pay for private schools that had the doors opened for their children. There were many philanthropic and charitable acts. Despite these noble initiatives and endeavours of many a Maltese and foreign person, both private and religious, it was not until the passing of the first *Compulsory Attendance Act* of 1924 that paved the way for a movement for the reform and up-dating of education.[1]

Although Education in Malta was not yet compulsory during the First World War, statements show the growth of the Elementary Schools during the period 1905–1906 to the period 1915–1916 from 15,698 (average number of scholars on registers) to 22,052 for the two periods respectively. The average attendance of scholars on registers showed an increase from 13,290 to 18,805 for the same periods. A return that showed the classification by age of the scholars attending Elementary and Infant Schools on 31 July 1915 gave a total of 19,655 children (boys and girls) aged less than 5 and over 14 (for Malta and Gozo).[2]

---

1   See also, *Education in Malta,* J. Zammit Mangion, 1992

2   *Report on the Elementary Schools' Department for 1915–1916*, Elementary Schools' Office, Malta, 20 April, 1916.

Young Maltese lads posing in British Military uniforms
(From a private collection)

The impact of the presence in Malta of so many sick and wounded affected Maltese society to the extent that these two children from Valletta aged 5 and 7 (boy and girl) are dressed as nurse and wounded for the celebration of Carnival Festivities! *(Courtesy of Mr Winston Zammit B.A. Hons. M.A.)*

11.2 The Church's Role

Archbishop Mawru Caruana was the head of the Maltese Church. The task faced by the Church was enormous in tackling the problems of poverty and squalor, which were being aggravated further by the war. The precarious situation of wartime precluded solemn celebrations.

In 1916, the people were much disgruntled by the rapid rise in prices. Moved by pitiful and miserable living conditions of the people, the Church took the initiative to present an appeal to the Governor. The Parish Priests met at St Francis Church in Valletta on 23 November 1916 and at 10.30 a.m. proceeded to the Palace where the petition was presented. They explained conditions in which the population were living and for the Governor to take the necessary measures to reduce the cost of living. The petition was read out in the presence of the Governor by Father Wigi Gatt O.P. Parish Priest of Our Lady of Porto Salvo Parish, Valletta.[3]

All the Corps of the Society of St Vincent also presented a petition complaining about the high price in bread and other essential commodities.[4]

In such difficult circumstances, the Archbishop felt the duty to help the needy and on 1 December 1916, set up a Committee under his auspices, which had the aim of collecting funds to help the poor in all their needs. All the presidents of the different Conferences of the Society of St Vincent were to form part of this committee, which had as its vice-President, the Auxiliary Bishop, Mons. Fra Angelo Portelli O.P.; Secretary, Mons. Guzeppi Depiro; Treasurer, Mr Fons Maria Galea and Mons Sidor Formosa as Member. The Archbishop also expressed his wish to have a collection organised in all churches for this purpose.[5]

---

3   *Malta Taghna*, 25 November 1916
4   *Ibid*, 2 December 1916
5   *Ibid.*, 9, December 1916

The Archbishop's appeal was well received and the money collection was encouraging. The Governor, on his part donated £100 and the Archbishop distributed £15 per month. The Chapter of the Cathedral donated £5 monthly, whilst Marchesa Scicluna donated £200. By the end of January 1917, £874 had been collected.[6]

A letter appearing in a local newspaper in December 1918, stated that about £5,000 had been collected, and during the period of two years more than £200 monthly.[7]

Another initiative, probably taken by the Church, were the Kitchens for the Poor organised in Rabat and Mdina run by a Committee, formed mainly by priests under the Presidency of the Parish Priest Dun Karm Sammut.[8]

The Government put the Parish Priests in charge of the distribution of flour to parishioners. An interesting and detailed list of how this distribution took place is found in 'Distribuzione Farina (1914–1918)'. An example of this responsibility is the Parish of St Julian's where, besides St Julian's, the territory entrusted to the Parish Priest of that time, (Dun Amabile Bonanno), included also Sliema and small parts of Birkirkara, Swieqi, Minsija, Imsieraħ, Gżira and St George's. All these fell within the parochial limits.[9]

It is interesting to note that due to the large number of war casualities in St Julian's and other areas, ecclesiastical authorities issued a circular ordering a lessening in bell ringing on 5 June 1915.

The reduction and subsequent complete stoppage of Church bell ringing was witnessed for the first time in Malta and was met with much disappointment as even the most solemn of Church

6   La Diocesi, Jan 1917, p246, Feb, 1917, p281–282, Mar, 1917 p. 295

7   Malta Taghna, 13 January 1917

8   La Diocesi Dec, 1917, pp. 219–220

9   See, San Giljan mitt sena parocca, 1891–1991: The centenary of a parish, St Julian's, Edited by Stanley Fiorini, 1992.

activities were without the peeling of bells. Feasts were celebrated in complete silence. For the first few months even the Viaticum was affected by this order. This had a cascading effect on Festas, as no fireworks or illuminations were permitted and the only sign of a Festa were the street decorations. It was only through a special permit that large lamps of the *Wagner* type were lit.

The British military authorities gave this order and the Church abided by it. It was thought that this order was effected, not only for the wounded that needed as much tranquillity as possible, but also because the echo of the ringing bells interfered with Wireless waves. This is understood in that Wireless was still in its infancy and such precautions were often taken, especially in times of emergency.[10]

The Church as seen in (section 11.1 of this Chapter) was also in the forefront in providing free education to children of poor families.

11.3 Government Assistance

In Malta, the war gave rise to a difficult situation, mainly because the Island needed to import the great bulk of its food requirement. As a result prices rocketed to new heights. The price of bread rose threefold (from 2d to 6d), of sugar fourfold (from 3d to 1s2d and meat three and a half times (from 1s to 3s6d).

To combat this increase in price the government exercised a certain amount of price control, and organised the distribution

---

10   *Il-Gbira Guerra tad-Dinja, Vol. IV*, Opra Colossali li tigbor fiha l-ahjar fattijet tal guerra mehuda minn fuk cotba ta potenzi nuetrali Propieta' Letteraria u Artistica ta Andolfo & Magro, Stamperija u Legatorija ta' Emilio Lombardi, 28, Strada Santa Maria, u 27, 28, Strada San Trofimo Sliema, pp. 2000–2001, 1924.

of foodstuffs by means of purposely set up Boards. A subsidy of £2,000 was also granted to millers to decrease the price of bread.[11]

Those employed on a fixed wage such as civil servants suffered terribly. Despite the dramatic rise in cost of living, the rates of salaries of the clerical establishment remained stationery or suffered a setback. The effects of malnutrition, were clearly visible on their families, and many clerks were compelled to withdraw their children from school and to surrender their life insurance policies.[12]

The Lieutenant Governor in the face of the sharp increase in price since August, 1914 addressed the sitting of the Council of Government on 22 December 1915:

"There are certain classes of people who have not been really adversely affected: commerce is not in a state of stagnation and happily there is little or no unemployment. However there is one class whether within or without the Government service which is feeling severely the increased cost of the plain necessity of life, and that is the class employed in many capacities at a modest fixed wage, a class whose necessary expenses have increased while its resources have remained stationery".

In these circumstances the Government decided to give a bonus of 10% on the salary to those employees who were earning £1 per week. For this purpose, the government voted £2,300 that was approved by the Council of Government in the same Sitting.[13]

Subsequently the Lieutenant Governor had this to say in December 1917.

---

11   *British Malta Volume II*, A Laferla.

12   *The Maltese Public Service 1800–1940: The Administrative Politics of a Micro-State, Godfrey* A. Pirotta, pp. 374–37, 1996.

13   *Debates of the Council of Government 1914–1917*, Vol. 28, pp. 174–175.

"As the war, however went on, the difficulties continued to increase and by January 1917, the situation had become almost desperate".

After the strike by the dockyard workers, the Government set up a Commission of Inquiry to investigate the reasons for the strike and also to examine the salaries of Government employees. The findings of the Commission clearly revealed that Government Civil Service employees were the least paid and in most cases the male breadwinners were receiving a salary less than is sufficient for the maintenance of their family. After examining the report, the Government decided to give a proportionate rise in salary to bread consumption of each family.[14]

For this purpose the Council of Government approved a Supplementary Vote of £9,600 as rebate on the price of bread to certain categories of Government employees and their dependents. The Lieutenant Governor's Office by means of Circular Number 4 of 1917 approved an arrangement for the grant of a rebate on the amount of bread consumed by certain categories of Government employees, (including teachers) and their dependents. The concession cancelled the War Bonus of 10% that was granted on 29 November 1915.

Employees not giving their full time work to the Government, and those serving with His Majesty's forces were not included in this concession. A Board appointed by the Governor was set up to deal with any question arising as to the applicability of the terms of this Circular in cases of doubt and Heads of Department were asked to submit to the Board detailed lists of employees in their Department coming within the scope of the Circular.

While the First World War was creating havoc and misery on most of the population, certain employees were profiting mightily

---

14   *Ibid.*, 1917–1921, Vol. 29 pp. 6–7

due to the heavy influx of servicemen. A typical example of this situation was the Union Club. The accounts for 1915 of the Club show a handsome profit in excess of £1,100. To their credit the committee decided to share some of this unexpected bonanza with the staff.

The staff's wages had remained unchanged since 1907. Buoyed by the unexpected extra revenue the committee decided to revise wages in line with the rise in the cost of living.

Apart from the wage increases themselves, the conditions of employment make fascinating reading. In particular those for waiters deserve singling out. These read:

Waiters coming on duty in the early morning may receive tea and in the evening after dinner the watch remaining (note the distinctly naval term) may receive what can be spared from dinner at the discretion of the secretary. Those on middle watch may receive tea. (The notion that staff would be fed on left-overs, if any, sheds further light on the world of the haves and have-nots of those days.)

Any breakages exceeding 2s. (10c) in any one month to be deducted from the employee's wages.

Wages in 1915 ranged from £1 a month to a maximum of £7 for the head cook. The club provided uniforms and shoes.

By 1916 the Great War had ground to a halt in the mud of Flanders. In Malta the effect was very secondary and apart from news received by telegram via Reuters the conflict had little impact on the life style of members with the club operating normally as in peacetime.

Pangs of conscience however prodded the Governor, Field Marshall Lord Methuen to direct his aide-de-camp Lieutenant Windsor to write to the club on 19 February 1916 as follows:

"His Excellency the governor with the concurrence of Vice Admiral sir Arthur Limpus, KCMG, Major General J. Barker, CB and Surgeon General H. Whitehead CB, begs to request the Committee of the Union Club to close the lower bar on and after Tuesday 22nd instant and further to give such instructions as may tend to restrict drinking at the Union club in Sliema.

The reason for His Excellency coming to this decision must be obvious to anyone who respects the good name of our country.

It is to be borne in mind that in the United Kingdom treating to liquor or spirits is illegal nor can any liquor or spirits be served in a club after 9.30pm".[15]

11.4 Health Awareness

The Public Health Department through the Chief Government Medical Officer issued numerous educational material in the form of health notices and other reading material to teachers and the population in general.[16] Circular 1/1918 issued on 12 January 1918 by the Director of Elementary Schools, Mr Reynolds (acting on instructions issued by the Chief Government Medical Officer), informed teachers about the period of exclusion of patients in the case of measles and whooping cough and mumps. A leaflet titled, *'Prevention of the spread of communicable diseases in schools'* had also been issued about this matter.

The Chief Government Medical Officer, Mr G. Caruana Scicluna of the Public Health Department issued a Notice dated 14

---

15 *The Malta Union Club, Newspaper Post,* July 2002. 'From the Archives, by Victor Cavallo, pp. 30–32

16 See also, *The British Fortifications, An Illustrated Guide to the British Fortifications in Malta,* Stephen C. Spiteri, 1991.

April 1917 about the occurrence in Malta of a few suspected cases of plague. He emphasised the importance that the public should know that rats and mice are very liable to contract the disease that is transmitted by fleas to other animals and also to man. Particular attention was requested for the cleanliness of dwellings by the frequent sweeping and washing of floors, so that fleas will find it difficult to live and multiply in dusty chinks and corners.

Another measure to combat the onset of disease was a Government Notice dated 12 June, 1917 where the Governor acting on the advice of the Council of Health made regulations whereby no accumulation of rags, tins, boxes, bottles and other articles that may afford harbourage for mice and rats was allowed to be kept in dwellings or other buildings or in their vicinity. This regulation could also be applied, at the Superintendent of Public Health, to ragstores licensed by Police Laws.

NOTICE.

IN view of the occurrence in these islands of a few suspected cases of plague, it is important that the public should know that rats and mice are very liable to contract the disease which is transmitted by fleas to other animals and also to man. In a time like this, rats and mice constitute a very great danger to the public health and their number should be reduced as much as possible.

Every householder should, therefore, adopt the following measures:—

a) rats and mice should be trapped or poisoned, and cats should be kept in places where these animals are generally observed.

b) any rat holes in buildings and yards should be filled up with broken glass and cement;

c) all domestic and kitchen refuse which invariably attracts rats and mice should be removed daily from dwellings and yards;

d) all unserviceable articles such as bundles of rags, old clothes, old bottles, empty tins and similar articles that are allowed to accumulate in yards, cellars, cupboards and in all odd corners, and which afford very good cover and breeding places for rats and mice, should be removed or destroyed at once;

e) particular attention should be paid to the cleanliness of dwellings by the frequent sweeping and washing of floors, so that fleas will find it difficult to live and multiply in dusty chinks and corners.

PUBLIC HEALTH DEPARTMENT,
Valletta, 14th April, 1917.

G. CARUANA SCICLUNA,
Chief Government Medical Officer and Superintendent.

AVVISO.

IN seguito allo sviluppo in queste isole di pochi casi sospetti di peste, è importante che il pubblico sappia che i topi e i sorci sono molto suscettibili a contrarre questa malattia, che, per mezzo delle pulci, viene trasmessa ad altri animali come pure all'uomo. In un'epoca come la presente i topi e i sorci costituiscono un gran pericolo per la salute pubblica, e il loro numero deve essere ridotto il più che sia possibile.

Ciascun capo di casa dovrebbe perciò adottare le misure qui appresso indicate:—

a) Trappolare o avvelenare i topi e i sorci, e tenere gatti ove i detti animali fossero generalmente osservati;

b) Otturare con tritume di vetro e cemento tutti i buchi che servono di nido ai topi nei fabbricati e nei cortili;

c) Rimuovere giornalmente dalle case e dai cortili tutti i rifiuti domestici e di cucina che sogliono immancabilmente attirare i topi e i sorci;

d) Rimuovere o distruggere subito tutti gli articoli inutili come cenci, indumenti vecchi, bottiglie vecchie, recipienti di latta vuoti e simili, accumulati nei cortili, nelle cantine, negli armadi e in tutti altri ripostigli della casa, che possano servire di nascondiglio e di nido ai topi ed ai sorci ;

e) Prestare cura speciale alla nettezza delle case, scopandone e lavandone con frequenza i pavimenti, in modo da rendere difficile alle pulci di vivere e moltiplicarsi nella polvere delle fessure e degli angoli della casa.

UFFICIO DI SANITA' PUBBLICA,
Valletta, 14 aprile, 1917.

G. CARUANA SCICLUNA,
Medico Principale del Governo e Soprintendente.

AVVIS.

BILLI chelna f'daun il gżejjer xi ftit casi sospetti tal pesta, hemm ħżonn illi uieħed għandu icun jaf illi il grieden u il firien huma uisk soggetti biex jieħdu din il marda u jaughxa lil animali oħrajn u lil bniedmin ucoll permezz tal brighed. F'żminijet bħal daun, il grieden u il firien huma ta periculu gbir għall sahhitna u chemm nistghu għandna nekirdu minnhom.

Cull cap tad-dar imela għandu jagħmel dan li sejrin inghidu:—

a) il grieden u il firien għandhom jinkerdu bin-nassi jeu bil velenu, u fil postijiet fejn hemm minnhom għandhom jinżamnu il ktates.

b) it-tokob tal grieden fil-djar u fil btieħi għandhom jiġu misduda bil frac tal ħġieġ u bis-sement.

c) il-żibel u 'l fdal tal chċina li il grieden jagħmlu għalih uisk, għandu jiġi imneħħi cull jum mid-djar u mill btieħi.

d) l-imbarazzi ta bla bżonn, bħal ma huma iċ-ċraret, huejjeg u fliexchen kodma, bottijiet vojta u huejjeg oħra li jinsabu migmugħin fil btieħi, fil cantini, ff'armarji u 'rkejjen oħra, u illi iservu biex biex il grieden jistaħbeu u ibejtu 'fihom, għandhom jitneħħeu jeu jinkerdu malajr.

e) uieħed għandhu jokod attent illi iżomm id-dar nadifa bil cnis u bil ħasil ta l'art biex il brighed ma isibux xkuk u irchejjen bit-trab li fihom jistgħu igħammru u jiżdiedu.

UFFICIU TAS-SANITA',
il Belt. 14 ta April, 1917.

G. CARUANA SCICLUNA,
Tabib Principali tal Gvern u Cap tas-Sanità.

Health Notice for the population (14 April 1917) in English, Italian and Maltese as a prevention against suspected cases of Plague

It was also stressed in the same Notice that the owner of any building was to keep in good state of repair the walls and floors of basements and the floors of yards and of ground-floors to prevent rats and mice burrowing into and forming runs in such buildings.

The Public Health Department issued a very detailed and extremely well illustrated Poster titled *Għandna Nibżgħu mid-Dubbien* (we should fear flies) in 1915 on the dangers posed by flies and their elimination and control.

As there were some cases of enteric fever in the Island, the Chief Government Medical Officer asked for the full cooperation of the Teachers in the Education Department (by means of a Memo dated 12 November 1917). In turn, the Director of Elementary Schools, Mr Reynolds asked Teachers and Instructors to explain the contents of a Poster that accompanied the Memo. He also instructed the pupils to tell their parents of the instructions contained in the said Poster with particular emphasis on the elimination and control of flies. This request was made, as the parents of children were mostly illiterate.

CHAPTER 12

WOMEN'S ROLE

Until 1883, men undertook nursing in the naval hospitals, usually ex-seamen or marines, who were recruited as required from the shore establishments and who held no nursing qualifications. An earlier experiment to introduce female nursing had generally proved unsuccessful and unpopular, though a few female nurses were still employed. A system of established and hired nurses was used in the naval hospitals: the former being entitled to a pension when they retired.

Regulations for the Staff of Nursing sisters in the Royal Navy Hospitals were published in 1884 and a female nursing service was established initially at Haslar (Portsmouth) and Plymouth. In 1897 the service was extended to Chatham and Malta, and in 1901 to all Royal Naval Hospitals.

The number of women serving in British Forces during the First World War is extremely small when compared to the number of men, but the role of women had been very strong and represented mainly in the caring sphere of activities.

According to the *Australian Bronze Commemorative Plaques Website*, in World War One, the Australian Army Nursing Corps had 2,692 Australian nurses who volunteered to serve in Australia, New Guinea, Egypt, Lemnos, Malta, Palestine, Mesopotamia, India, Northern Greece, England, France, Belgium, Italy, Russia and hospital ships and troop transport ships on the high seas. 25 nurses died on active service.[1]

Women who saw service in the British Forces (and ancillary units) served mainly in the following areas:

---

1   See *www.plaques.satlink.com.au*

- *Women's Army Auxiliary Corps (WAAC) later Queen Mary's Army Auxiliary Corps* (This was established in Spring of 1917).
- *Women's Royal Naval Service* (WRNS)
- *Women's Royal Air Force*
- *Queen Alexandra's Imperial Military Nursing Service.*

The Women's Royal Naval Service (WRNS) was established in November 1917 and a request had been made for the Navy to share the WAAC. As no speedy response was forthcoming, the Navy decided to form their own branch of female service. Dame Katharine Furse became Director of the formation (she had previously been Commandant of the British Red Cross Voluntary Aid Detachments).

At its peak there were 438 officers and 5,054 ratings employed by the WRNS. They were scattered widely in the United Kingdom being heavily employed in all the main naval ports and destinations as widely scattered as Anglesey and the Orkneys. Foreign postings were also possible, with the initial destination being Gibraltar. WRNS also served in Malta and Genoa but plans to deploy them more widely in the Mediterranean area were thwarted by the end of the War. The WRNS were disbanded on 1 October 1919.[2]

Major Maurice Micallef Eynaud very well expounds the generous and unselfish contribution of Maltese women in a feature titled '*Nurse of the Mediterranean*':

> **"Maltese ladies organised tearooms in Sliema and Valletta, entertainment in hospitals and elsewhere, and car and motor-launch excursions. They met each hospital ship on arrival in all weather and at all times, distributing refreshments and parcels of tobacco, matches, stationery, etc., to the wounded.**

---

2   *Imperial War Museum, Information sheet No. 38*: The Women's Royal Naval Service in the first World War, 2001.

A large sewing party augmented limited hospital supplies by providing pyjamas, shirts and socks for the patients....everal Maltese ladies, not to be outdone by their men folk joined the VAD (Voluntary Aid Attachment) and were assigned to various military hospitals where they gave a good account of themselves. Two of them, Mary Muscat and Violet Briffa were mentioned in Despatches for their singular devotion and duty in Mtarfa and Cottonera hospitals respectively.

The Marchesa Scicluna generously lent her beautiful residence Villa Dragonara, as a convalescent home for 20 officers, and donated £100 monthly towards its upkeep."[3]

In any estimate of what Malta gave in the war in terms of facilities for the sick and wounded, one should also include houses lent for hospital purposes. An example of this generosity is Villa Dragonara, (mentioned above) which was granted by the Marchesa Corinna Scicluna O.B.E as a convalescent home. This lady was an illustration of generosity and her name stands high in the long list of Maltese ladies who give themselves to patriotic service in the war, as do, those, of Mrs Bonavia, M.B.E. and Mrs Mifsud M.B.E.

The Staff of the Elementary Schools Department also contributed £50 to the Ladies' Fund of he Order of St John and British Red Cross; nearly £18 was also contributed by Rev. J. Grech S.J. and Mr Busuttil, Inspector of Schools, which were proceeds of lectures given in schools by them.

The Staff also collected and contributed 48,300 cigarettes, 934 cigars, 215 pipes, 2,300 oranges and lemons, 700 sticks, besides

---

3   See *Sunday Times (Malta)* of 1 December 2002 Feature on p55 written by Major Maurice Micallef Eynaud. Major Micallef Eynaud wrote this feature with grateful acknowledgment to Professor Victor G. Griffiths, for use of his material. Major Micallef Eynaud also contributed another feature titled; 'The Cottonera Military Hospital', in the *Malta Independent on Sunday* of 21 December 2003. also where, amongst other things, he mentioned the contribution of Maltese ladies in alleviating the suffering of the wounded.

smaller quantities of cigarette paper, matches and chocolates. The Mistress and elder girls made up 3,500 garments and other articles including pyjamas, towels, bags, operating suits and overalls. Eight assistant teachers served in the St John Ambulance Association Brigade for ambulance work, for periods varying from six to eleven months, whilst thirty-seven female teachers obtained the St John Ambulance Association Certificates in First Aid and Home Nursing.

Maltese women also played a significant part at home in the preparation of bandages for use in hospitals. This home work was also a source of additional income to the household.[4]

12.1 Medical Missionaries of Mary and the Malta Connection

(by Sister Isabelle Smyth)[5]

John A. Mizzi notes the following of the Gallipoli campaign:

"Few episodes in the battle annals of the British Empire can match the nine-month Gallipoli campaign for waste of life of rank and file, for valour, suffering, endurance and loyalty on land, sea and, for the first time, in the air and for indecision and incompetence in the leadership and ill-luck in the military sphere. The two contending sides faught face to face and chest to chest and died like the flies that fed on their unburied bodies."[6]

Gallipoli and its Malta connection played a significant part in shaping the world view of the young Marie Martin. These events painted the backdrop against which would soon begin to emerge

---

4   Information made available by Mr Winston Zammit M.A.

5   his feature has been taken from the *Yearbook of the Medial Missionaries of Mary*, Healing & Development, 2002 Edition, pp. 24–30

6   *The Gallipoli campaign: The Malta Connection*, John A. Mizzi, 1991.

her awareness of the call to establish the Medical Missionaries of Mary.

Early in August of 1914, Britain, France and Russia were drawn into what had started as a local war between Serbia and Austria-Hungary, and which eventually involved 32 nations. It was naively thought that this would be 'the war to end all wars'.

Ireland was still under British rule, and while conscription only applied on the mainland, many young Irish men volunteered for service. Tommy Martin, Marie's older brother, had graduated from Trinity College, Dublin, and went to the war with the Connaught Rangers. A younger brother, Charles, aged 20, was still an undergraduate, but gave up his studies and trained with the Royal Dublin Fusiliers at the Curragh Camp.

The changing times made a big impact on the young women too. Marie Martin, then aged 23, applied to join the Voluntary Aid Detachment (VADs). Later, her younger sister, Ethel, and her aunt, Lily Moore, did likewise. Marie was immediately accepted and sent for three months' training to the Richmond Hospital in her native city, Dublin.

The Voluntary Aid Detachment, founded in 1910 as an emergency volunteer reserve, was a division of the British Red Cross. It was indeed as a home defence unit to be mobilized only in case of invasion. Two-thirds of the volunteers were women. VADs have been called 'Roses of No-man's-land' and 'Lilies of the Field'. But these young women who left comfortable homes to perform the most menial of nursing duties – in crowded hospitals and First Aid Stations whose patients were horrifically wounded and maimed – had courage stronger than steel.

In July 1915 Charles Martin's regiment sailed for Gallipoli, arriving at Suvla Bay on August 7. This campaign had been badly devised from the start. The planned invasion of Turkey from the

Marie Martin (right) with colleague and patients, January 1916

Marie Martin 1915

Malta, December 1915. Marie Martin (right) with her friends Miss Jenkins and Miss Paul.

Gallipoli peninsula was aimed at diverting Turkish forces from the pressure they were putting on the Russians. Success would provide a direct ice-free supply line to Russia via the Black Sea. At the same time, the Gallipoli campaign was seen as an opportunity to open a new 'theatre of war' as an alternative to the stalemate that had developed on the Western Front – with both sides entrenched along a 500-mile stretch from the border of Switzerland to the North Sea.

In February 1915 the British and French navies had attempted an invasion of the Gallipoli Peninsula from the narrow straits known as the Dardanelles on the north-western coast of Turkey. They suffered terrible defeat. Again in April, this time supplemented with Australian and New Zealand ground forces, the loss of life was tremendous, with little to show for it. In August, a new major offensive was begun.

The Mediterranean island of Malta, like Ireland, was under British rule in those days. At the outbreak of the war, Malta had four small hospitals with a total of 118 beds. Its quick-thinking Governor, Lord Methuen, ordered the expansion of existing hospitals and the selection of buildings suitable for conversion. A scheme was drawn up to extent the number of beds to 2,000 on the island of Malta, with a further 500 beds for convalescents at Fort Chambray on the adjacent island of Gozo.

Initially it was expected that those sent to Malta would be only slightly wounded, just needing convalescence before returning to the warfront. But the landings at Gallipoli's Suvla Bay were accompanied by a rising tide of sickness, which was to ravage the troops even more than enemy wounds. Dysentery and enteric fever put huge demands on the emergency services throughout the summer of 1915. As these decreased with the onset of the winter, they were replaced by trench fever and frost-bite.

In those months, Malta managed to convert several barracks, schools and even two Governor's palaces providing 28 hospitals with a total of 20,000 beds at the peak of the emergency. During this peak period, the average bed occupancy was 16,004. By January 1916, Malta had 334 medical officers, 913 nurses (including VADs) and 2,032 rank and file members of the Royal army Medical Corps.

Lieutenant Charlie Martin was wounded at Suvla Bay, but not seriously enough to be sent home. Two months after he had sailed for Gallipoli, Marie was called up for service with the VADs in Malta. Her mother accompanied her to London where they spent a week together before Marie joined the hospital ship *Oxfordshire*. The ship had 250 beds, but at times carried as many as 550 wounded men.

On October 22, 1915, they reached the harbour of Malta's capital, Valletta. They were a day earlier than expected so their assignments were not ready. Marie, a city girl who loved social life, was delighted when they were allowed ashore for three hours. She and her pals were anxious "to see as much as we can in case we are banished to the other side of the island". They explored Valletta and "had tea, and deadly rich cakes". This was probably at Blackleys where she returned on other occasions when she got her half-day off duty. Next day she was assigned to a converted barracks on a peninsula overlooking St George's Bay, on the northern shore of the island, about six or seven miles from Valletta. It had opened as a hospital on May 6th. Beds at St George's Hospital numbered 840 when Marie arrived but were increased to 1,002 in November.

Dr G.R. Bruce, Specialist Sanitary Officer in Malta, reported as follows:

"St George's Hospital occupied a large area, since the majority of wards were small, holding that time 10 patients each; consequently the staff, considerably under numbers at first, had to work under great difficulties. As at most of

the other hospitals, the sick soon predominated over the wounded at St Georges."

Dr Bruce also noted "…the new staff, however willing, were mostly without experience of the work and necessary routine of military hospitals. However, this deficiency was largely discounted by the great zeal and enthusiasm shown by all concerned, regardless of regular meals and sleep, and it was remarkable how soon the staff became efficient in their new roles".[7]

That zeal and enthusiasm was shared by Marie Martin, the youngest of the VADs who had sailed on the *Oxfordshire*. She wrote to her mother on October 28 saying, "The work is really hard, but of course it is what we came out for." A letter of November, 25 said " I am just as happy as I can be on duty and I only wish I had two pairs of arms and legs to be able to do twice a much".

In one letter home she reported that she had "about 120 beds to make each day. Sheets are scarce an the dysentery is appalling." In another, she was caring for 140 patients, many of them with broken backs. Her time off, she said, went on sleep or writing letters for very ill patients. When a patient died, she would write to his mother with details of his final days.

October brought mosquitoes and sand flies that left her face in a terrible state and her eyes swollen. Sometimes the sirocco wind was strong. Days were hot and airless. But by December, it had become cold, and in the pouring rain they were drenched going from ward to ward.

Whenever she could, Marie would make her way to the convent chapel of the Blue Sisters in St Julian's for Mass or Benediction. She told her mother, in a letter of November 7, that the Reverend Mother at the Blue Sister' hospital would like her to be transferred

---

7   *Military Hospitals in Malta during the War*, G.R. Bruce, MA, MD, Capt. RAMC

there. Life would probably have been somewhat easier in this well-established hospital where Officers were cared for, but Marie would not ask for any such special privilege.

She was very excited when she got her first ever pay packet. The yearly salary for a VAD was £20, as well as board and uniform. She carefully registered a letter to her mother with one pound and five shillings saying, "It is not very much but perhaps by Christmas I shall be able to save a little more for you and then you could buy yourself something nice you want. I wish I could only earn enough to make things easier for you. Always let me know how things are going at home. I pray every day that you my have no more worries or troubles."

Evidently this widowed mother of twelve children confided her worries, both economic and otherwise, to Marie, her eldest daughter.

Unlike other nurses and VADs, Marie did not take part in off-duty social life in the company of the Medical Officers. But many of her letters home enquired with concern for a special friend called Gerald Gartland who was also serving in the war. She anxiously looked out for letters from him or news of his safety and whereabouts.

Naturally, she was concerned for her brother Tommy, who had been wounded and sent back to Ireland where he was convalescing on Bere Island. She wrote to Tommy on November 26, hoping he would not be sent on active service for a while. She asked him if there was "any sign of this terrible war ending?"

Tommy was ordered abroad again the following February, to the Egyptian port of Alexandria. But meanwhile, as 1915 drew to a close, more worrying news came of Charlie. By early December there was talk of a withdrawal from Gallipoli. The terrible death toll from this campaign already exceeded a quarter of a million young lives on each side. Marie wrote home saying the latest batch of patients from the Dardanelles told her there was so much fighting at Gallipoli, but no troops had been withdrawn yet, so she presumed Charlie was still there. However, in the week ending December 9th, the number of casualties landed at Malta was 6,341.

While doing the dressings a lot of news was exchanged. Patients told her conditions were terrible where they had been. Most had frost-bite. On December, 18 she wrote that one young boy among a new convoy of patients told her he had seen Charlie very well about two weeks earlier. She promised her mother that next day she would contact the Wounded Bureau on the island to find out if any of the new arrivals were from the Royal Dublin Fusiliers. They might have more news of Charlie.

As Christmas approached, with all the other staff, Marie was busy trying to get the wards decorated and presents ready for the patients. She was off duty just in time to attend Christmas Midnight Mass at St Patrick's Church Sliema, a glorious night, and after it, they had to walk most of three miles or so back to St George's.

On December 27, Marie received a cable from her mother saying the War Office had notified her that Charlie had been wounded and was missing. Very distraught, Marie redoubled her efforts in search of news of her dearly loved young brother. She hoped against hope that he might yet arrive on one of the hospital ships. The Medical Information Bureau in Malta frequently appealed to the patients for news of comrades seeking them for any information at all on lists of men reported missing. But on December 29 with a heavy heart, Marie had to write home saying there was no news in Malta of Charlie's whereabouts.

The New Year of 1916 dawned. On January 4, she wrote home again saying she had been trying hard to get news. The people she met at the war Office were very kind. She had phoned Salonika, but the only news there was that Charlie had been wounded between

5th and 11th December. She had one and a half days off duty and wrote from Dowdall's Hotel where she had gone with a nurse friend *"to think and rest and make enquiries"*.

The weeks passed with little news. An Officer who was a patient at the Blue Sisters' Hospital told her that Charlie had been slightly wounded in the arm on December 6th. On January 24th, she wrote home saying it seemed likely he had been taken prisoner.

By then, all the Allied troops had been evacuated from Gallipoli – the authorities having decided to abandon any further attempt to capture Constantinople by that approach. Work slackened in Malta.

On February 6th she could report that she had met several men from Charlie's regiment. They knew he had been wounded on December 7th and again on December 8th, after which he and about a hundred others went missing. They were sure he had been taken prisoner. They all thought very highly of Charlie. He always used to say, *"What's good enough for the men is good enough for me to get on with"*.

A few days later, Marie met two Officers who explained that there was only one road off the hill Charlie had been on, so it was most likely he had been taken prisoner.

March came, still no definite news – until, at last, Marie came across a patient who had actually seen Charlie being wounded in the leg on December, 8th. He told her the Bulgarians had captured the whole trench and marched them away. He was sure Charlie had not been killed.

All of this was taking its toll on Marie, and by March she was longing for home. Four days later she wrote saying she had met another patient who had been with Charlie when he was wounded. This man gave this young Officer great praise for having held up the advance, making retreat possible. He was sure Charlie was a prisoner.

Marie continued her search for information. In April she went out to St David's Camp, where she met another man who was in Charlie's Company. He told her Charlie had been giving orders on the parapet and was wounded badly through the shoulder. He was with them for fifteen miles when they had to retreat. Then the Bulgarians captured him and about thirty others. This man himself felt lucky to have escaped.

Work in Malta was very slack by now. Marie's six-month contract was ending. In her last letter from Malta, she said who knew there was more to be done in France.

Marie left Malta on Holy Thursday, which fell on April 20th in 1916. The journey home took two weeks including several days in London. She was still on her way home, when, on the following Monday, April 24th, the Eater Rising begin in Dublin. Life in Ireland would never return to the pre-war world she had known.

A month later, Marie was called up again for service, this time at Hardelot in France. Just a few miles south of them, the First Battle of the Somme began on July 1st, and would claim 800,000 lives before it ended in December. They could hear the firing at the Front and ambulances were ferrying in convoy after convoy. At one point, for four days she had to care for 56 stretcher cases suffering from gas poising, with only one orderly to help her.

It was in Hardclot on July 2nd that Marie received news from her mother saying she had been informed that Charlie had died of his wounds two days after his capture on December 8th. His death had come just one week after his 21st birthday.

Marie's six-month contract in France ended just before Christmas of 1916. Later for a brief period in 1918 she would again serve as a VAD, this time in an English convalescent hospital at Leeds.

Marie spent the whole of 1917 at home. As she reached her 25th birthday she began to make a serious discernment about her future. She prayed much. Gradually, it became quite clear, at least in broad outline. She wrote "*Next day I went to meet my friend. I wore my new navy suit and white spots I told him that for me marriage was out of the question. But as yet I did not know what to do*".

That was the beginning of a long twenty years of following a persistent yet uncertain dream. Before long it would bring her to Nigeria where she witnessed at first hand the need for a medical congregation of religious sisters. Then came years of ill health and other obstacles before eventually on April 4th 1937, she made her vows while very ill in a government hospital in Port Harcourt, Nigeria. At that moment MMM was born. She became known as Mother Mary Martin. When she died in 1975, the Congregation she had founded had grown to 450 sisters. Today MMMs come from 18 different nationalities and work in 16 countries.[8]

---

8   "When Irish eyes are smiling I am coming back to you. Little maiden of the mountains with your bonnet eyes of blue."
(From a popular song, which I, as author of this book dedicate to Mother Marie
     Martin)

CHAPTER 13

AFTERMATH AND CONCLUSION

13.1 Political Scenario

On the international arena, the scene was set for a gradual revival of Germany, which in 1918 had been deprived of the heavy industrial capacity when the Rhineland (the heart of German industry) had been placed under Allied control. The expansionist policy of Germany and its rearmament were menacing Europe with a wider world conflict that was witnessed between 1939 and 1945. The Second World War lasted nearly six years and was waged by 56 nations and cost well over 50 millions lives. It was indeed the most violent and prolonged conflict that mankind has ever experienced to date.

This book has reviewed Malta's role in the following main aspects:

- Hospital for wounded servicemen
- A dockyard for the British Navy
- An internment camp for prisoners-of war
- The service given by Maltese soldiers, sailors and airmen in different campaigns such as Salonika, Gallipoli and the Western Front.

The story of Malta in the Great War is one of a well-organised and responsive society, that had its hands full of war-work of one kind or another centrally placed, not immune from danger of air-raids and bombardment (as shown in Chapter 4, dealing with Aviation). It was entirely secure because of the sea-power of the British Empire with which Malta had cast in her lot

Against the background of the above important roles, the Maltese social and political scenario was much agitated and the

Maltese blood ran strong in the Maltese nation's veins in search for self-governance and an improvement of not only in social and political rights but also in the cost and standard of living which had reached rock bottom.

Ref. Malta Government Gazette , January, 1920.   Page 10

Anno Domini 1920.

PROCLAMATION(() isembodyment of KOMRM and RE(Militia) Malta Division

By His Excellency Field Marshal Lord Plumer , Knight Grand Cross of the Most Honourable Order of the Bath, Knight Grand Cross of the Most Distinguish Order of Saint Micheal and Saint George, Knight Grand of the Royal Victoria Order, Colonel York and Lancashire Regiment , Governor and Commander in Chief in and over the island of Malta and its Dependences and Commander of the Troops serving within the same.

Whereas on the fifth day of August , 1914, a Proclamation was issued by the Governor and Commander in Chief in these islands, under the provision of Article 5 of Oedinance No. XI1 of 1901 , ordering the embodiment of the King's Own Malta Regiment of Militia and the Royal Engineers (Militia) Malta Division , from the said date and until further Orders, in consequence of the existance of a state of War between His Majesty the King and a foreign Power.

And whereas it is provided by article 8 of the said Ordinance that it shall be lawful for the Governor and Commander in - Chief to order by Proclamation , that the Royal Malta Regiment of Militia , now known as the King's Own Malta Regiment of Militia and the Royal Engineers (Militia) , Malta Division shall be disembodied.

Now, therefore, in exersice of the powers confered on Me as aforsaid , I do hereby order that the said King's Own Malta Regiment of Militia and the Royal Engineers (Militia) Malta Division , shall be disembodied not later than the 31st. day of January 1920.

The Palace Valletta. this 16th day of January, 1920.

By Command,

(Sgd)   W. C. F. Robertson

Lieut: Governor
and Chief Secretary to Goverment.

Demobilisation 16 Jan 1920 Disembodiment of KOMRM and Royal Engineers (Militia)

The inevitable growth of working class militancy, especially in the harbour and dockyards and the public service where masses of workers came together led to the establishment of workers organisation to develop. Initially these started off as of the mutual benefit type. But as the crises ran deeper many workers especially in the dockyard and the civil service went on to set up their unions and associations based on and affiliated to the British trade union movement.

Between the years 1889 and 1903, the climax in infrastructural works in Malta had reached a high peak. Thanks to politicians in the mould of *Gerald Strickland* (1861–1940, who was Principal Government Secretary, many valuable services were introduced in Malta such as gas lighting in the streets, drainage, and the building of many schools. Many politicians accused him of serving the British needs and not the Maltese and interfering too much in the day-to-day affairs of the running of the country.

He was also accused of building schools as large as hospitals as if in preparation of war to accommodate the wounded. As for his efforts in developing a drainage system, it was said that his ideas in this matter would only bring about a spread of disease. To quell the political dissent, Strickland was very effectively led to become governor of the Leeward Islands in the West Indies between 1902 and 1904, Tasmania (1904–1909), West Australia (1909–1912) and New South Wales (1912–1917).

In 1917 Strickland returned to Malta and started opposing the proposed succession duty. His opposition of direct taxation helped to boost his popularity. The Nationalists were all out against him and tried their best to obstruct his political comeback.

Another politician, *Enrico Mizzi* (1885–1950) strived hard to obtain a liberal Constitution, and for this he was arrested and court martialled on charges of sedition in 1917 (under the Malta defence regulations) for writing against the British. He was sentenced to a year's imprisonment with hard labour, the loss of civil rights and the withdrawal of lawyer's warrant. The sentence was commuted by Governor Methuen to a 'severe censure', whiles his civil rights and warrant were restored following the cessation of hostilities in 1918.[1]

A document reviewing the measures, which were being taken during 1919 to alleviate the economic and living conditions of the poorest people of the Islands, made reference to the administrative structure of the Government during the War. Particular reference was made to the contagious diseases that reached epidemic proportions in Malta during the war years. It praised the Public Health authorities of their efforts to combat this situation, which in other countries wrecked havoc. In the process, it commended also their policies, which helped to control diseases in a highly dense population that was badly malnutritioned.[2]

The Maltese population felt aggrieved by the low standard of living and high cost of living, which could barely allow them the bare means of living. Salaries were a rock bottom level and many Maltese found themselves demobilized and without the prospect of a job. All these factors plus the high rate of illiteracy and lack of proper compulsory education meant that most of the workers had to emigrate to hope for a better life mainly in Australia and the United States.

During the whole war period about 80,000 wounded and sick Allied officers and men were cared for in Malta, many of them – estimated at 20,000 – being from the Australian expeditionary Force at Gallipoli. In Malta there are 204 graves of Australians who died

---

1   *Maltese Biographies of the Twentieth Century*, Michael Schiavone and Louis Scerri, 1997 and *Towards Responsible Government, Historical Background of Constitutional Developments up to 1921*, by Dr R. Farrugia Randon M.D. FR. Hist. S. (Lond) which appeared in the Report and Accounts of the Mid-Med Group of 1993.

2   Information by courtesy of Louis Henwood kindly made available from his website at *http://louishenwood.com/history/no29.html*

in the First World War, in Malta. The Australian Government did not reciprocate Malta's kindness to the Australian sick. In August 1916, the Australian government placed a virtual prohibition on Maltese immigration because of pressure from the labour movement, which regarded the Maltese as 'cheap labour', and the White Australian racists who regarded the Maltese as 'black' or semi-white'. It was not until 1944 that the Australian Government placed the Maltese on the same immigration footing as other 'White British Subjects', according to the official terminology.[3]

13.2 The Spanish Flu

The Spanish Flu or as it is commonly known in Maltese *'L-Ispanjonla'* was an influenza pandemic of 1918–1919 that killed more people than the Great War. The figure of dead is somewhere between 20 and 40 million people. The magnitude of this epidemic also known as *'la Grippe'* is the most devastating in world history. Its killing effects were greater than the Bubonic Plague of the 12th Century. Indeed a global disaster that cost the lives of so many young people. Amongst the severe complications arising from this flu was pneumonia.

As hostilities were nearing the end in autumn of 1918 a new enemy was looming on the horizon to spread death for both friend and foe on the opposing battlefronts, as well as on the civilian population. The Journal of the American Medical Association in its final edition of 1918 noted the following:

"1918 has gone: a year momentous as the termination of the most cruel war in the annals of the human race: a year which marked, the end at least for a time, of man's destruction of man; unfortunately a year in which developed a most fatal infectious disease causing the deaths of hundreds of

3   *Journal of the American Medical Association* of 28 December 1918

thousands of human beings. Medical science for four and one-half years devoted itself in putting men on the firing line and keeping them there. Now it must turn with its whole might to combating the greatest enemy of all – infectious disease."[4]

13.3 Rioting and Self-Government

Apart from the rampant infectious diseases, the end of the war brought about many other social ills and political upheavals as witnessed by the riots of 7 June 1919 in Valleta when British troops opened fire on the Maltese demonstrators.[5]

The root causes leading to this event were the scarcities of essential commodities for the population. The Government faced a series of economic ills: demobilisation and unemployment, budget deficit, and high prices that brought so much suffering on the population Trade unionism was taking a firm hold by spreading worker militancy. Dissent was further aggravated by a Constitution that did not allow political representation and decision-making by the Maltese in their daily affairs.

Unemployment was rampant, especially for the unskilled worker. The fear of a run-down of the labour force employed at the Drydocks was high. Already, in 1919 many people had been redundant due to demobilsation. Also 4,000 Maltese soldiers that had been recruited in the Labour Battalions that served at Mudros, Taranto and Salonika during the war were demobilised.

---

4   *Journal of the American Medical Association* of 28 December 1918

5   The four Maltese civilians killed were **Karmnu Abela, Guzeppi Bajada, Wenzu Deyer and Manwel Attard**. The victims died on 7 June 1919 except for Karmnu Abela who succumbed to his wounds in hospital on 16 June 1919. Their names appear on a monument erected in their memory at the Adolorata Cemetery where they lay to rest.

During the war, the Maltese population suffered much due to scarcity in essential supplies. Many imports of wheat, flour, oil, cheese, meat sugar, paraffin, wood and other essential commodities did not reach Malta due to 'The Unrestricted Marine Warfare' of the German Imperial Navy.

At the end of hostilities in November 1918, the Maltese were expecting a decrease in the prices and an increase in supply, being aware that in other countries bread had benefited from price cuts and the provision was quite abundant. The expectations of betterment in the standard of living conditions were in the people's minds. This awareness was further accentuated by the daily newspapers of the time: *Daily Malta Chronicle, Malta Herald and Malta*.

In 1919, Malta witnessed a heavy influx of Russian refugees escaping the horrors of the Russian Revolution. The fleeing Russians tried and to some extent managed to earn a small measure of income by using their skills to sell Russian delights

Malta achieves self-Government
(Courtesy: Malta Independent)

(sweets) and other typical Russian products in order to safeguard their livelihood in an already below the poverty line environment.

The increase in importation taxes in 1917 and the introduction of the Entertainment Tax on cinema attendance and the Succession and Donation Duties caused much fuming and fretting among the Maltese, so much so that even the Church and the high-income classes of the population showed their indignation against such measures.

The increase in wages did not compensate for the increase in the cost of living. Another factor that caused much disgruntlement was that the British did not allow the Maltese to administer their internal day-to-day affairs and there was a demand from Maltese politicians for a Constitution that allowed self-government.

The development of trade unionism in Britain and elsewhere

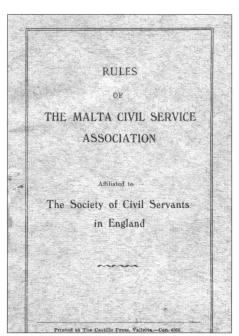

as well as the increase in mass unemployment at the Drydocks (from 4,000 at the start of the war to 12,000 at the end of hostilities) led to the possibility of the setting up of a trade union. Worker consciousness about the British counterparts receiving a much higher salary for the same type of work performed by the Maltese aroused much frustration and a feeling of exploitation amongst the Maltese workers that reached a peak high on 7 June 1919.

The war left in its wake a nation seeking reforms at the highest level, to meet the needs of the working population. The absence of fundamental and substantive social and political rights was manifested by economic depression at the end of Britain's belligerency. The wars brought much employment and abundance and distracted the Maltese from any change. But the end of hostilities re-surfaced the birth pangs of the nation dependent wholly on war for its living.

Malta was granted responsible government in 1921 to calm the signs of unrest. Its working was not totally to the satisfaction of the British, and Malta reverted to the status of a Crown Colony in 1936.

First meeting of the Assemblea Nazionale
(Courtesy: Malta Independent)

CHAPTER 14

THE MILITARY HERITAGE

It is a pity that many, if not most of the buildings and sites connected with wartime Malta (and which constitute a local and tourist attraction) have been abandoned or reduced to ruins. The artistic and historical value of most military appreciation is only limited and confined to picturesque and vivid descriptions found in tourist brochures or specialized publications on military architecture and fortifications.

The farther back one delves into history, the greater the probability that the more pitiful is the state of repair and abandonment of such sites. Private and public agencies exist and do their utmost to take initiatives to create awareness and initiate concrete steps to ameliorate, if not totally restore such sites. The State on its own part is, invariably duty bound to preserve our heritage.

The First World War has now long gone and its memory lies in the many military cemeteries that are the resting place of so many war dead. As indicated above, most of the other sites connected with this period of the British military period are either crumbling into ruins, (a classical and typical case is the Australia Hall in Pembroke) and may only be viewed from a distance. In themselves they constitute a danger to life and limb and accessibility is a risky business. Others are being used by private or public institutions such as the Cottonera Hospital, which houses St Edward's College or Zammit Clapp Hospital, which is a specialized hospital for the elderly. Other areas are used by Government agencies such as Bighi Hospital are used to house the Malta Restoration Centre.

The Malta Tourism Authority that falls under the responsibility of the Ministry for Tourism has created a map to give the user

A selection of heritage sites and museums

an overview of the military architecture and suggests routes and sites to visit. The intention of the map is to fill a void in heritage promotion in this field. The map also refers the users of the map to several publications which deal specifically with Malta's military architecture and fortifications during the period of the Knights of Malta period (1530–1798) and the British Period (1800–1964).[1]

The Tourist Information Centre in Valletta also compiled a list of army/navy airforce cemeteries that may be viewed by the public. For the benefit of the reader and with the kind permission of this office the said list is being reproduced hereunder. Other lists of forts, fortresses, regimental barracks, batteries, redoubts, military hospitals, war graves, airfield and other military installations are also being reproduced from the above-mentioned map. This map also gives a key to the accessibility to these sites in three levels (Easily Accessible, Access limited and Remains only).[2]

14.1   Army/Navy/Airforce Cemeteries

- **Pembroke Military Cemetery**: This cemetery is situated between St Andrew's and what was formerly St Patrick's Barracks. A bus service normally runs close to the cemetery from both Valletta and St Paul's Bay.
- **Pietà Military Cemetery**. This cemetery is about 1.5 kilometers away from Valletta and is approached by the main road going to Sliema. It can be reached by any bus going to Sliema and the north of Malta.

---

1   Malta achieved independence on 21 September 1964. Successive agreements, between the Maltese and British Governments, allowed for a limited British military presence in Malta up to 31 March 1979.

2   I am indebted to the management and staff of the Tourist Information Office that falls under the auspices of the Malta Tourism Authority for taking time to find the right source of information for my research. As for the army/navy/airforce cemeteries, the Malta Tourism Authority indicated Mr Peter Fitzgerald (cemetery commissioner) for further information on these cemeteries.

- **Mtarfa Military Cemetery**. This cemetery is about 1.2 kilometres away from Rabat. A direct bus service from Valletta is available
- **Kalkara Naval Cemetery**. This is also known as Capuċċini Cemetery and is about a mile southeast from Rinella, close to the Capuchin convent. It belongs to the Admiralty. This cemetery can be easily reached by bus from Valletta
- **Air Force Memorial** in Floriana near car park
- **A Commonwealth Memorial** can also be found in Floriana
- **Naval memorials** can be found at the Msida Yacht Marina and Kalkara gardens in Floriana.

List of Military Sites according to Region

Region 1

- Fort Tignè
- Fort Tignè Barracks
- Brennan Torpedo Launching Ramp, Tignè
- Garden Battery
- Fort Cambridge
- Fort Sliema (Fortizza)
- St George's Barracks
- Pembroke Battery
- Fort Pembroke
- Pembroke Camp
- Pembroke (P.O.W.) Chapel
- St Andrew's Barracks
- St Andrew's Hospital
- St Patrick's Barracks
- St Patrick's Cemetery
- Wardija Battery and Field Defences

- Fort Campbell
- Mellieħa Cemetery
- Mellieħa Ridge Defences (Infantry trenches)
- Fort Mellieħa (Civil Defence Depot)
- Għajn Tuffieħa Baracks & Firing Ranges

Region 2

- Victoria Lines – N.W. Front
- Fort Madalena
- San Giovanni Battery
- Għargħur High Angle Battery
- Sound Mirror –Maghtab
- Nuclear Underground Command Centre
- Fort Mosta
- Tarġa Battery
- Connaught Hospital, Mdina
- St David's Barracks – Mtarfa
- Mtarfa/Ta' Qali Cemetery
- Mtarfa Hosptial
- Dewjra Lines
- Fort Binġemma
- Fomm Ir-Riħ Redoubt

Region 3

- Kalkara Cemetery
- Bighi Hospital
- Fort Ricasoli
- Fort Ricasoli Barracks & Brennan Torpedo ramp
- Fort Rinella
- Fort St Rocco
- Della Grazie Battery

- Fort San Leonardo
- Żonqor Battery
- St Paul's Battery
- Fort tas-Silġ
- Wolseley Battery
- Fort Delimara
- Delimara Lighthouse
- Fort St Lucian
- Fort Bengħisa
- Wied Żnuber Stop Wall and Field Defences
- Ħas-Saptan Underground fuel Depot

Region 4

- Fort Manoel
- Quarantine Lazzaretto
- Ta' Braxia Cemetery
- ANZAC Graves
- San Salvatore counterguard (Milorda Gardens)
- Floriana Bastions Cemetery
- Floriana Barracks
- Lintorn Barracks
- Fort St Elmo
- Upper St Elmo Barracks
- Lower St Elmo Barracks
- Sacra Infermeria
- Lascaris Battery
- Maria Addolorata Cemetery
- Corradino Lines
- St Clement's Retrenchment
- Fort Verdala
- Verdala Barracks

- Royal Naval Bakery
- Fort St Angelo

14.2 Gozo

- Fort Chambray Cemetery
- Signalling Tower – Nadur
- Ġordan Lighthouse

14.3 Airfields

- Kalafrana, Sea Plane Base
- Ħal-Far
- Safi
- Qrendi
- Luqa
- Ta' Qali
- St Paul's Bay, Sea Plane Base
- L/O Għajnsielem, Gozo

14.4 Commemorative monuments and plaques

- The Upper Barrakka, Various – Valletta
- The Lower Barrakka, Ball's Monument – Valletta
- World War II Memorial and Siege Bell monument – Valletta
- St Paul's Anglican Cathedral, Various – Valletta
- St Andrew's Scots Church, Various – Valletta
- The Cenotaph (War Memorial), – Floriana
- The R.A.F. Memorial – Floriana
- The R.M.A Memorial – Floriana
- The K.O.M.R. Memorial – Floriana
- St Publius Church Memorial – Floriana

- World War II Monuments at, Żabbar, Tarxien, Sliema, Cospicua, Żebbug
- Manoel Island Memorial – Manoel Island
- Yacht Marina Submariners Memorial – Msida
- Cenotaph – It-Tokk, Victoria, Gozo.

14.5 Museums and AV Displays

- War Museum – Valletta
- War Rooms, Lascaris – Valletta
- Maritime Museum – Vittoriosa
- Wartime Experience – Valletta
- Aviation Museum – Ta' Qali
- Gozo Heritage – Għajnsielem, Gozo
- Malta Experience – Valletta

APPENDIX A

List of KOMRM and RMA Officers (1914–1918)

Name	Unit	Appointments, promotions and Overseas Service
Adair J.	KOMRM	5
Agius Joseph R.	KOMRM	5
Agius L.	KOMRM	2, 3
Agius A.	KOMRM	5
Amato Gauci Edgar	KOMRM	2, 5
Amato Gauci Attilio	KOMRM	RAF
Amato Gauci R.	KOMRM	6
Arrigo Anthony	KOMRM	2, 5
Aspinall J. V.	KOMRM	2, 5
Bencini Robert	KOMRM	2, 7
Benjacar Alfred	KOMRM	6
Bezzina (Dominican)	Chaplain	Salonika Labour Corps 7
Boffa	Medical	Salonika Labour Corps 7
Bonella W. L.	KOMRM	6
Bonello J.V.C.	KOMRM	6
Bonavita John.	RMA	1, 3
Bonnici J.L.	RMA	3
Borg S.	RMA	3
Briffa A C.M.G.	KOMRM	2, 5
Briffa de Piro E.J	KOMRM	2, 5
Briffa H.	KOMRM	5
Briffa J.H.	KOMRM	5
Busietta E.L	KOMRM	6
Busietta C.A.	KOMRM	6
Busutill E.D.	KOMRM	6
Busutill J.	RN	Reserve
Calleja Schembri G.	RN	Reserve
Cauchi	Chaplain	Salonika Labour Corps 7
Carbonaro O.M..	RMA	1, 3
Cardona A.G.R.	RMA	3
Caruana C.	RMA	3
Caruana G.	RMA	1, 3

Name	Unit	Appointments, promotions and Overseas Service
Caruana L.	KOMRM	6
Camilleri J.	RMA	3
Cavarra J.E.	KOMRM	2, 5
Camilleri C.J.	KOMRM	6
Chappelle J.V.	KOMRM	6
Chappelle V.	KOMRM	6
Curmi H.	KOMRM	6
RMA		6
Cutajar Zammit	KOMRM	2
Calleja Schembri	KOMRM	Chaplain 2, 6
Dandria A.	KOMRM	2, 5
Darmanin J.E.	RMA	3
Demajo Albanese	RN	Reserve
De Domenico J.M.O	RMA	1, 3
De Piro J.E.	KOMRM	3
RMA		6
De Piro W.W. H.	KOMRM	6
Denaro F.	KOMRM	5, 2
Denaro C.A.	RMA	1, 3
De Giorgio C. L	KOMRM	6
Falzon Sant Manduca	RMA	1, 3
Ferro H.W.	KOMRM	2, 5
Ferro C.H.	KOMRM	2, 5
Flery A.S.	RMA	3
Ganado A.W	RMA	1, 3
Ganado W.C.	RMA	1, 3
Gatt W.R	RMA	1, 3
Gatt A.J	RMA	1, 3
Gatt E.A.	KOMRM	2, 5
Gatt J.	KOMRM	6
Gera W.	KOMRM	6
Grech H.A	KOMRM	6
Gollcher Frank	KOMRM	6
Gouder Carbone S.	RMA	1, 3
Huber Herbert W.	KOMRM	2, 7, 9
Huber Edgar	KOMRM	6, 9

Name	Unit	Appointments, promotions and Overseas Service
Illiff P.	KOMRM	2, 5
Jackson H.L.	KOMRM	6
Jackson H.A.T.	KOMRM	RAF
Laferla A.V.	KOMRM	2, 5
Laferla H.G.	KOMRM	2, 5
Leonardini J.	KOMRM	2, 5
Kelly J.	KOMRM	2
Magri J.V.	KOMRM	6
Magri J.A.	KOMRM	6
Mallia A.V.	KOMRM	6
Manche' C.	KOMRM	2, 6 (Medical Doctor)
Manduca P.	KOMRM	6, 7
	RAF	2
Micallef H.W.	KOMRM	3
	RMA	3
Micallef V.C.	RMA	2, 5
Micallef A.E	KOMRM	2, 5
Micallef H.G.	KOMRM	2, 5
Micallef Eynaud A.W.	KOMRM	Munster Fusilliers
Micallef Eynaud Alfred	KOMRM	2, 6, 7, 9
Mifsud Edward A.	KOMRM	2, 5
Mifsud J.	KOMRM	2, 5
Mifsud E.	RMA	1, 4
Mizzi R.	RMA	1, 3
Montalto F.	KOMRM	6
Muscat C.A.	KOMRM	
	S.Staff	2, 5
Muscat P.	RMA	1, 4 (Chaplain)
Muscat J.	KOMRM	5, 7
Nicosia J.	KOMRM	6
Pace Charles	KOMRM	2, 5
Pace J.L.	RMA	3
Pratt A.S.	KOMRM	2, 6
Psaila Manche' J.	KOMRM	5
Randon R.	RMA	1, 4
Reynaud E.H.	RMA	1, 3

Name	Unit	Appointments, promotions and Overseas Service
Rizzo V.	RMA	3
Salomone J.	RMA	1, 3
Sammut Leonard.	KOMRM	6
Sammut P.	KOMRM	2, 6
Samut R. M.D.	KOMRM	2, 6 (Chaplain)
Samut Tagliaferro S.	KOMRM	2, 6, 7
Sant Cassia F. Count	KOMRM	2, 5, 7
Savona W.	RMA	1, 3
Savona P.	RMA	1, 3
Savona E.	RMA	1, 3
Sciortino C.E.	KOMRM	2, 5, 7
Semini A.J.	RMA	1, 3
Speranza E.R.	RMA	3
Stivala Frank	KOMRM	2, 5, 7
Tabone J.A.	KOMRM	6
Terreni J.	KOMRM	6
Testaferrata Bonici P.	KOMRM	2, 5
Testaferrata Oliver H.	KOMRM	5
Torregiani J.C.	KOMRM	6
Torregiani C.	KOMRM	2, 5
Teuma Castelletti J.	KOMRM	2, 5 (Contino, Col. A.D.C)
Trapani A.	KOMRM	2, 5
Trapani V.A.	KOMRM	6
Vassallo C.	KOMRM	2, 5
Vella W.D.	RMA	1, 3
Vella R.	RMA	1, 4
Vella C.D.	KOMRM	2, 5
Vella H.D	KOMRM	2, 5
Vella E.J.	KOMRM	2, 5, 7
Von Brockdorff U.	KOMRM	2, 5, 7
Von Brockdorff C.	KOMRM	5, 7
Von Brockdorff H.	KOMRM	5
Xuereb C.A	KOMRM	6

Appendix B

The Register of the names (Maltese and Gozitan – Seamen only) of those who fell in the years 1918–21

*The names of these men have come to the author's knowledge from other sources, notably the Government Gazette of 19 November, 1938 which lists the Maltese roll of honour for the Great War.

Extracted from Index No M.R.2

Abela Carmelo   Fireman HMS *Louvain*   Age 47
Husband of Agostina Abela
of 28, Strada Carmine, Casal Żabbar, Malta.

Agius Giuseppe   Fireman HMS *Louvain*   Age 29
Son of Michele and Teresa Agius,
of 6, Strada Sant. Angelo, Sliema.

Agius John   Trimmer HMS *Louvain*   Age 18
Son of John and Eliza Agius
of 44, Halsafline St, Casal Paula.

Agius Lorenzo   Seaman HMS *Louvain*   Age (n/a)
Husband of Carmela Agius
of 29 Strada Loggia, Casal Paula.

Arnaud Giuseppe   Stoker HMS *Louvain*   Age 35
Son of Carmelo and Catarina Arnaud (nee' Aquilina) of
Tripoli: husband of Onorata Arnaud (nee' Aquilina)of 91
Strada Santa Scolastica, Vicolo 2DO, Vittoriosa.

Attard Battista   Fireman HMS *Chesterfield*   Age 51
Son of Francesco and Vincenza Attard; husband of Carmela Attard,
of 61, Sda San Lazzaro, Cospicua.

Attard Francesco   Fireman HMS *Louvain*   Age 18
Son of Luigi and Angela Attard.
of 27 Strada Santa Domenica, Victoria, Gozo.

Azzopardi Giorgio   Trimmer HMS *Sarnia*   Age (n/a)
Son of Francesco and Paolo Azzopardi,
of Victoria St Vicolo

Bartolo Angelo   Fireman HMS *Louvain*   Age 37
Son of Anthony and Maria Bartolo, of Nadur, Gozo.

Bonello Lorenzo   Leading Stoker HMS *Louvain*   Age 32
Son of Francesco and Filomena Bonello of Senglea; husband
of Federica Bonello of 68 Strada Punta, Senglea.

Bonnici Paolo   Trimmer HMS *Louvain*   Age 37
Son of Salvatore and Teresa Bonnici; husband of Maria Carmela
Bonnici of 35 Strada S. Domenico, Casal Żabbar.

Borg John   Cook HMS *Louvain*   Age 33
Son of Lorenzo and Anni Borg; husband of Lucarda
Borg of 17 Strada San Gaetano, Ħamrun.

Borg John   Fireman HMS *Chesterfield*   Age 26
Son of Emmanuele and Guiseppa Abdilla of 3 Strada Torri, Msida.

Briffa Gio Maria   Trimmer HMS *Louvain*   Age 41
Son of Felice and Anna Briffa; husband of Maria Briffa,
of 186 Strada Church Avenue, Casal Żabbar.

Brincat Rosario   Trimmer HMS *Sarnia*   Age 50
Son of Andrew and Annie Brincat, of 50 Strada San Guiseppe, Casal Luca.

Calleia Assuero   Fireman HMS *Louvain*   Age 47
Son of Pacifico and Paola Calleia; husband of
Giovanna Calleia of 32 Strada Lia, Żabbar.

Camilleri Emmanuele   Trimmer HMS *Louvain*   Age 26
Son of Alexander and Anny Bugeja Camilleri. Born at Żejtun.

Camilleri Giorgio   Fireman HMS *Louvain*   Age 33
Son of Luigi and Catarina Camilleri (nee' Dimech) of Żejtun; husband
of Catarina Camilleri (nee' Callus) of 19 Strada Paolo, Żejtun.

Carabott Francesco   Trimmer HMS *Louvain*   Age (n/a)
Son of Lorenzo and Catarina Carabott (nee' Marmara'); husband
of Esther Carabott, of Strada Giardino Botannico, Żejtun.

Carabott Gaetano   Trimmer HMS *Louvain*   Age 36
Son of Lorenzo and Catarina Carabott; husband of Consiglia
Carabott of 26 Strada Buon Consiglia, Casal Żejtun.

Cassar Carmelo   Stoker 1st Class HMS *Louvain*   Age 27
Son of Giovanni and Guiseppa Cassar of Żejtun; husband
of Carmela Cassar of 82 Strada Reale, Żejtun.

Cerami Paolo   Officer's Steward 1st Class HMS *Louvain*   Age 29
Son of Antonio and Antonia Cerami of 70 Strada
Brighella, Ħamrun, Born at Valletta.

Chircop Paolo   Stoker 1st Class HMS *Louvain*   Age 28
Son of Carmelo and Carmela Chircop; husband of Lorenza
Chircop of 212 Strada Manderaggio, Valletta.

Cini Carmelo   Trimmer HMS *Louvain*   Age (n/a)
Other family details n/a

Curmi Emmanuele   Stoker 1st Class HMS *Louvain*   Age 23
Son of Salvatore and Giovanna Curmi; husband of
Carmela Curmi of 2, Strada Porrenti Valletta.

Cuschieri Guiseppi   Trimmer HMS *Sarnia*   Age (n/a)
Son of Joseph and Lorenzo Cuschieri of Casal Burin, Sda. Sebastiano.

Cutajar Alfonzo   Trimmer HMS *Louvain*   Age 48
Son of Andrea and Giovanna Cutajar of Cospicua; husband of
Caterina Tabone Cutajar of 106, Strada Sammat, Casal Paula.

Cutajar Francis   Able Seaman HMS *Louvain*   Age 30
Son of Giuseppe Cutajar and Teresa Darmanius, his wife; husband
of Maria Cutajar of 66 Strada San Lorenzo, Vittoriosa.

Davis George   Electrical fitter HMS *Louvain*   Age 38
Son of Joseph and Julia Davisof 7, Strada Sperone, Valletta.

Debattista G.*   Electrical Fitter HMS *Louvain*   Age n/a
Other details are not available

Debono Michele   Trimmer HMS *Louvain*   Age 29
Son of the late Lorenzo Debono of Malta; husband of Paula
Debono of 58 Strada S. Antonio, Casal Attard.

Degiorgio Salvatore   Able Seaman HMS *Louvain*   Age (n/a)
Other family details n/a.

Dimech Joseph   Officers' Cook HMS *Louvain*   Age 23
Son of Antonio Dimech of 42 Hassafliene St, Casal Paula.

Edwards Giuseppe   Trimmer HMS *Louvain*   Age 24
Son of Joseph and Giovanna Edwards of Strada Regina, Casal Paula.

Ellul Eligio   Fireman HMS *Louvain*   Age 35
Son of Giuseppe and Maria Ellul; husband of Marta
Ellul of 28 Strada Magazzini, Floriana.

Ellul John   Assistant Engineer HMS *Louvain*   Age 26
Son of Peter Paul and Ethel Ellul of 4, Sda. Kirscia, St Julian's.

Endrich Giovanni   Stoker 1st Class HMS *Louvain*   Age 27
Son of William and Lunziata Endrich of Senglea; husband of
Guiseppina Endrich of 69, Strada Bastione, Senglea.

Falzon Carmelo   Greaser HMS *Otranto*   Age(n/a)
Son of George and Antonia Falzon of 63 Strada San Patrizio, Valletta.

Falzon Francesco   Trimmer HMS *Louvain*   Age 21
Son of Michele and Maria Falzon of 24 Strada
Hondok ir-Rummien, Kala, Gozo.

Farrugia Gaetano   Trimmer HMS *Louvain*   Age 23
Son of Spiridione and Barbara Farrugia of 81 Strada San Trofimo, Sliema.

Farrugia John   Fireman HMS *Louvain*   Age 40
Son of Francesco and Medalina Farrugia of 1
Idaolo Pieta, Vicolo Terzo Valletta.

Farrugia Domenico   Stoker 1st Class HMS *Louvain*   Age 24
Son of Spiro and Vincenza Farrugia (nee' Chircop) of Valletta; husband
of Margherita Farrugia of 300 Strada Manderaggio, Valletta.

Fenech Carmelo   Assistant Canteen Manager HMS *Louvain*   Age 34
Son of Carmelo and Michelina Fenech of Valletta; husband of
Marianna Fenech of 5 Strada Dietro La Chiesa, Sliema.

Formosa Angelo   Trimmer HMS *Louvain*   Age 31
Son of Carmela Formosa and the late John Formosa.
of 62 Strada Lampuca, Casal Paola.

Galea Paolo   Assistant Steward HMS *Louvain*   Age 18
Son of Vincent and Mary Galea of 49h Fleur de Lis, Birchircara.

Galea Spiridione   Fireman HMS *Louvain*   Age n/a
Other family details n/a.

Gauci Giovanni   Able Seaman *'Frigate Bird'*   Age 19
Son of Antonio and Vincenza Gauci of 81 Sda. Hamri, Ghainselem, Gozo.

Grech Salvatore   Fireman HMS *Louvain*   Age 29
Son of Vincenzo and Maria Grech

Grima Emmanuele   Fireman HMS *Louvain*   Age 30
Son of Guiseppe and Teresa Grima.

Grima Salvatore   Able Seaman *'Frigate Bird'*   Age 36
Son of Francesco and Teresa Grima of Kala, Gozo; husband
of Angela Grima of 123 Strada Wardia, Kala Gozo.

Grioli Joseph   Officers' Steward 1st Class HMS *Louvain*   Age 40
Son of Gaetano and Filomena Grioli; husband of
Concetta Grioli of 83 Strada Levante, Valletta.

Lia Carmel   Stoker 1st Class HMS *Louvain*   Age 20
Son of Joseph and Michelina Lia, of Senglea; husband
of Margherita Lia, of 39, Strada Punta Senglea.

Magri Antonio   Trimmer HMS *Louvain*   Age 32
Son of Paolo and Antonia Magri of Tarxien; husband of
Marianna Magri of 45 Annunziata St, Tarxien.

Mangion Joseph   Fireman *'Vitol'*   Age n/a
Other family details n/a

Meilak Salvatore   Fireman HMS *Louvain*   Age 28
Son of Vincent and Emilia Piott Meilak; husband of Maria
Dolores Meilak of 52 Strada Torre San Giovanni, Vittoriosa.

Meli Carmelo   Able Seaman HMS *Louvain*   Age 23
Son of John Meli of 22 Strada Mezzo Giorno, Casal Żabbar.

Micallef Carmelo   Cook HMS *Louvain*   Age 46
Son of Giachino and Maria Fava Micallef; husband of Giovanna
Ellul Micallef, of 149 Strada Reale, Casal Żabbar.

Micallef Giovann   Cook HMS *Louvain*   Age 24
Born at Valletta; son of Henry and Mary Borg
Micallef, of 4, School Street, Ħamrun.

Micallef Tancar   Assistant Cook HMS *Louvain*   Age n/a
Other family details n/a

Mifsud Emmanuele   Stoker 1st Class HMS *Louvain*   Age 34
Son of Joseph and Michelina Mifsud of Żejtun; husband
of Lorenza Mifsud of 46 Strada Taltas, Żejtun.

Muscat John   Assistant Engineer HMS *Louvain*   Age 29
Son of Vincenzo and Teresa Muscat; husband of Marianna
Muscat of 6 St Paul's Square, Ħamrun.

Natoli Saviour   4th Engineer HMS *Gazelle* killed
                            in action in HMS *Louvain*   Age 19
Son of Francis and Caterina Natoli of 96 Sda. San Lucia, Valletta.

Pace Emmanuele   Fireman HMS *Louvain*   Age 32
Son of Carmelo and Carmela Pace; husband of
Marianna Pace of 11 Strada Seconda, Floriana.

Parnis Annungiato   Trimmer HMS *Louvain*   Age n/a
Son of Valentino and Margarita Parnis

Pisani Michele   Officers' Steward 1st Class HMS *Louvain*   Age 47
Son of Carmelo and Maria Pisani of 117, Strada San Gaetano, Ħamrun.

Portelli Antonio   Fireman HMS *Louvain*   Age 33
Son of Vittoria and Paolino Portelli; husband of Filomena
Portelli of 15 Strada san Patrizio, Valletta.

Portelli Carmelo   Trimmer HMS *Louvain*   Age n/a
Other family details n/a

Sant Lorenzo   Fireman HMS *Louvain*   Age 33
Son of Carmelo and Rosaria Sant.

Sant Salvatore   Able Seaman *'Frigate Bird'*
Son of Giuseppe and Carmela Sant of 43, Sda. Hamri, Ghainsielem, Gozo

Schiavone Giuseppe   Stoker 1st Class HMS *Louvain*   Age 22
Son of Felice and Carmela Schiavone of Porto Salvo, Senglea.

Speranza Antonio   Seaman HMS *Louvain*   Age 25
Son of Costantino and Rosina Speranza; husband of
Emmanuela Speranza of 11 Strada Nuova, Pietà.

Spiteri Joseph   Assistant Steward HMS *Sarnia*   Age n/a
Other family details n/a.

Spiteri Carmelo   Stoker 1st Class HMS *Louvain*   Age 26
Son of Angelo and Guiseppa Spiteri; husband of Francesco
Spiteri of 28 Strada San Giovanni, Cospicua.

Spiteri Giovanni   Stoker 1st Class HMS *Louvain*   Age n/a
other family details n/a.

Stafrace Guiseppe   Fireman HMS *Louvain*   Age 27
Son of Giovanni and Grazia Stafrace; husband of Rosaria
Stafrace of 51 Strada San Nicola, Valletta.

Stivala Carmelo   Fireman HMS *Louvain*   Age 40
Son of Luigi and Giuseppa Stivala; husband of
Maria Stivala of Strada Fosso, Vittoriosa.

Tanti Emmanuele   Stoker 1st Class HMS *Louvain*   Age 47
Born at Valletta; son of the late Paolo Tanti and Vincenza Spiteri;
husband of Giuseppa Tanti of 31 Strada Porta Marina, Senglea.

*Tabone S.   Steward HMS *Louvain*   Age n/a
Other details not available

Vella Angelo   Fireman HMS *Louvain*   Age 45
Son of Pubblio and Maria Vella; husband of Giovanna
Vella of 31 Broad Street, Hanrun

Vella George   Officers' Cook 1st Class HMS *Louvain*   Age 32
Son of the late Antonio and Giovanna Vella; husband of
Giuseppa Vella of 127 Strada Reale, Ħamrun.

Williams Alfred   Leading Stoker HMS *Louvain*   Age 23
Son of George and Angela Williams; husband of Giuseppa
Williams of 44 Strada San Guiseppe, Valletta.

Xerri Carmelo   Seaman HMS *Louvain*   Age 29
Son of Michael and Carmela Xerri; husband of Rosina Xerri.

Xiberras Guiseppe   Officers' Steward 1st Class HMS *Comet*   Age 40
Son of Giovanni and Rosina Xiberras; husband of Maria
Xiberras of 40 Strada Santa Maria, Ħamrun.

Xiberras Guiseppe   Able Seaman '*Frigate Bird*'   Age 38
Son of Giovanni and Rosa Xiberres of Xeuchia, Gozo; husband
of Maria Xiberres of 2, Strada Gharus, Xeuchia, Gozo.

Xuereb Carlo   Officers' Cook 2nd Class HMS *Louvain*   Age 42
Son of Michele Angelo and Vittoria Xuereb; husband of
Rosaria Xuereb of 10, Strada Reale, Ħamrun.

Xuereb Salvatore   Trimmer HMS *Louvain*   Age 37
Son of Benedetto and Maria Xuereb of 31 Strada Taltas, Żejtun;
husband of Maria Xuereb of 31 Strada Tatlas, Żejtun.

Zahra Emanuele   Fireman HMS *Louvain*   Age32
Son of Lorenzo and Maria Antonia Zahra; husband of
Carmela Zahra of Strada Fleur-de-Lis, Birchircara.

Zammit Carmelo   Leading Stoker HMS *Louvain*   Age 30
Son of Paolo and Elizabetta Zammit; husband of Carmela
Zammit of 92 Strada San Guiseppe, Valletta.

Appendix C

Hospitals and Convalescent Depots: 1914–1918

Hospital	Date of Opening	Beds on First Day	Beds at Full Expansion	Date of Closure
Cottonera	Pre-war	167	802	Post War
Imtarfa	Pre-war	55	1853	Post War
Forrest	Pre-war	20	186	Post War
Valletta	Pre-war	36	524	Post War
Tigné	2.5.15	600	1314	6.5.19
St George's	2.5.15	840	1412	31.10.17
St Andrew's	9.5.15	1172	1258	-
Dragonara++	14.5.15	12	20	29.8.17
Blue Sisters	6.6.15	80	120	30.6.17
Floriana+	9.6.15	600	1304	30.4.17
Ħamrun	10.6.15	108	117	5.7.17
All Saints*	12.6.15	1465	2000	11.17
Baviere	15.6.15	105	155	14.8.17
St Ignatius	2.7.15	155	196	-
Sisters', Floriana	10.7.15	12	31	15.3.16
St David's+	25.7.15	464	1168	1.5.17
St Elmo	12.8.15	218	348	10.17
St Patrick's+	15.8.15	1000	1168	24.4.17
GħajnTuffieħa*	15.8.15	2000	5000	1.19
St Paul's+	25.8.15	240	898	27.4.17
St John's	1.9.15	400	520	9.10.17
Fort Chambray*	4.10.15	400	400	13.3.16
Manoel	5.11.15	500	1184	21.12.18
Spinola+	6.11.15	1000	1168	27.4.17
Ricasoli	6.11.15	800	800	19.2.16
Mellieħa*	20.11.15	1250	2000	5.9.17
Verdala++	9.12.15	30	30	17.4.16
San Antonio++	8.1.16	50	50	19.3.16

Legend: +Convalescent Depots, ++Convalescent Homes, *Staff transferred to Salonika
Source: *Gallipoli: The Malta Connection*, John Anthony Mizzi 1991, p. 132 (published by courtesy of the author).

Appendix D

List of Gozitan servicemen killed in the Great War

Il-Qala

1. **Attard Giovanni Battista**, son of Guzepp of 40, Triq l-Imgarr. Stoker. Died on HMS *Chesterfield* on 18 May 1918.

2. **Attard Nikola**, son of Antonio of 13, Triq in-Nadur. Sailor. Died on HMS *Rosario* on 18 August 1917.

3. **Buttigieg Guzepp**, husband of Marija, of 5, Triq l-Imgarr. Malta Labour Corps (n.2802). Died in Salonika between September and November 1918.

4. **Debono Anglu**, son of Francesco of 37, Triq in-Nadur. Sailor. Died on the Merchant Ship SS *Gladpuin*.

5. **Debono Salvatore**, son of Grezzju, of 35, Triq Wileg. Malta Labour Corps (n. 129). Died in Salonika between September and November 1918

6. **Demanuele Mikiel**, son of Guzepp, of 42 Triq Hondoq. Sailor. Died on the Merchant Ship SS *Rosario* on 18 August 1917

7. **Falzon Francesco**, son of Mikiel, of 24 Triq Hondoq. Trimmer (n. 3277). Died on HMS *Louvain* on 20 January, 1918.

8. **Grima Salvatore**, husband of Angla of 23, Triq il-Wardija. Sailor (n. 85974). Died on HMS *Frigate Bird* on 11 March 1918.

9. **Portelli Carmelo**, son of Pawlu, of 52 Triq l-Imgarr. Sailor (n.6318). Died on HMS *Louvain* on 20 January 1918.

10. **Thewma Mikiel**, son of Guzepp, of 2 Triq il-Kuncizzjoni. Malta Labour Corps (n. 4274). Died in Salonika between September and November 1918.

Għajnsielem

1. **Cassar Carmelo**, son of Spiru, of 21 Triq Hamri. Malta Labour Corps. Died in Salonika between September and November 1918.
2. **Cauchi Loreto**, son of Pietru of 63 Triq Hamri. Malta Labour Corps. Died in Taranto.
3. **N.B. By mistake, his name appears on the War Memorial erected in honour of the Gozitan victims of the Second World War at it-Tokk, Gozo.**
4. **Gauci Giovanni**, son of Anton of 81 Triq Hamri. Steward. Died on HMS *Frigate Bird* on 11 March 1918.
5. **N.B. For some unknown reason his name appears on the War Memorial erected in honour of the Gozitan victims of the Second World War at it-Tokk, Gozo.**
6. **Grima Giovanni**, son of Dionisia, of 12 Triq il-Knisja. Malta Labour Corps. Died in Salonika between September and November 1918.
7. **Sant Salvu**, husband of Carmela, of 22 Triq Gamri. Sailor. Died on HMS *Frigate Bird* on 11 March 1918.

   N.B. By mistake, his name appears on the War Memorial erected in honour of he Gozitan victims of the Second World War at it-Tokk, Gozo.

8. **Vella Lawrenz**, husband of Assunta of 18, Triq Hamri. Died on the Merchant Ship SS *Mavisbrook* on 17 May 1918.

Ir-Rabat

1. **Attard Francesco**, son of Angelica, of 20 Triq San Duminku. Trimmer (n. 36277). Died on HMS *Louvain* on 20 January 1918.
2. **Bugeja Guzepp**, son of Francesco of 35 Triq San Gwann. Malta Labour Corps. Died between March and May 1917.

3. **Cefai Salvatore**, brother of Grezzju, of 3 Triq Għajn Qatet. Malta Labour Corps (n. 4409). Died in Taranto.

4. **Gatt Carmelo**, husband of Marija, of 30 Triq San Duminku. Malta Labour Corps. Died in Salonika between March and May 1917.

5. **Gatt George**, son of Giovanni, of 90 Triq Palma. Malta Labour Corps. Died in Salonika between March and May 1917.

6. **Gauci Eugenio**, son of Censu of 42 Triq Putirjal. Malta Labour Corps. Died in Salonika between March and May 1917.

L-Ghasri

1. **Attard Carmelo**, son of Wigi of 6 Triq Wilga. Malta Labour Corps. Died in Taranto.

2. **Camilleri Mikiel**, son of Karmnu, of 9 Triq il-Misrah. Sailor. Died in Malta on a Minesweeper.

3. **Camilleri Salvu**, husband of Marija of 5 Triq il Kanun. R.A.F.(n. 83). Died in Taranto.

4. **Saliba Wigi**, son of Pawlu, of 1 Triq il-Kanun. Malta Labour Corps. Died in Salonika between March and May 1917.

San Lawrenz

1. **Axiaq Ignazio**, son of Salvu of 42 Triq San Lawrenz. Malta Labour Corps. Died in Salonika between September and November 1918.

2. **Mizzi Carmelo**, son of Tereza of 18 Triq il-Wileg. Malta Labour Corps (n. 550). Died in Salonika between September and November 1918.

Ta' Kercem

1. **Cassar Giovanni**, husband of Tereza of 45 Triq Santa Lucija. Malta Labour Corps (n.995). Died in Salonika between March and May 1917.

Ta' Sannat

1. **Sacco Guzepp**, husband of Roza of 20 Triq Saguna. Malta Labour Corps. Died in Salonika between March and May 1917.

In-Nadur

1. **Attard Pawlu**, son of Saverio, of 33 Triq Xandriku. Steward (n. 25435). Died on HMS *Shark* on 31 May 1916 during the Battle of Jutland.
2. **Bartolo Anglu**, son of Marija of 15 Triq tas-Sajd. Fireman (n. 808). Died on HMS *Louvain* on 20 January 1918.
3. **Camilleri Francesco**, son of Ganni of 2 Triq Grunju. Private, K.O.M.R of Militia. Died in a Hospital at Cambridge, circa. November 1918.
4. **Camilleri Mikiel**, son of Guzepp of 33 Triq Dun Grezz. Fireman (n. 21671). Died on the Merchant Ship, SS *Stuart Prince* on 22 March 1917.
5. **Camilleri Salvu**, son of Mikilel, of 19 Triq il-Knisja. Malta Labour Corps. Died between September and November 1918.
6. **Grima Anglu**, son of Mikiel of 16 Triq it-Tigrija. Fireman. Died on the ship SS *Landover Castle* on 27 June 1918.
7. **Mejlaq Guzepp**, son of Marija, of 13 Triq Grunju. Malta Labour Corps (n. 578). Died in Salonika between September and November 1918.
8. **Tabone Salvu**, son of Giovanni of 28 Triq Grunju. Steward (n. 32518). Died on the Merchant Ship SS *Shimosa* on 30 July 1917.

Ix-Xagħra

1. **Galea Giovanni Battista,** husband of Carmel, of 2 Triq Għajn Qamar. Sailor (n. 1335). Died on HMS *Canopus* in the Dardanelles. His son, Anton died during the Second World War serving as a sailor on the ship SS *Chelsea* on 30 August, 1940.
2. **Spiteri Guzepp**, son of Pawlu of 20 Triq Parsott. Malta Labour Corps. Died in Malta.
3. **Sultana Guzeppi,** son of Marija, of 12 Triq Gorf. Malta Labour Corps. Died in Taranto.

Ix-Xewkija

1. **Azzopardi Carmelo**, son of Carlo, of 13, Triq l-Imgarr. Malta Labour Corps. Died in Taranto.
2. **Bigeni Publio**, son of Francesco, of 3 Triq San Bert. Sailor (n. 13797). Died on a Hospital Ship.
3. **Xuereb Guzepp**, son of Giovanni of 35 Triq Sant'Indrija. Malta Labour Corps. Died in Salonika between March and May 1917.

APPENDIX E

First World War Relief Funds

The first two funds shown below were set up through private philanthropic initiatives, whilst the third fund was established by the Church.[1]

1. National Relief Fund in Aid of Local Charities – Distressed Families[2]

Closure of Fund	Account of Operations
Receipts	£698-17-9
Disbursements	£698-17-0

2. Lady Methuen's Fund for Distressed Families[3]

Amount collected	£860-18-4

3. Archbishop's Bread Fund

This fund was established in December 1916:

Funds Collected in Dec. 1916 – September 1917[4]	£2393-10-0
Distributed in Bread Tickets	£1692-0-0
Funds Collected till 28 March, 1918[5]	£3298-4-0
Funds Collected till 31 July 1918[6]	£4167-18-5

---

1   Mr Winston Zammit B.A (Hons) M.A. has researched the information supplied in these funds who kindly made it available for publication.

2   *Daily Malta Chronicle* 25 September 1917

3   *Ibid.*, 5 April 1918

4   *Ibid.*, 13 October 1917

5   *Ibid.*, 3, April 1918

6   *Ibid.*, 31 July 1919

Winding-up of Fund[7]
Amount Collected till 14 December, 1918   £4828-14-1
Amount Collected till 20 January 1919   £5000-0-0

The amount of suffering alleviated during the past two years has been great, 598, 394 bread and soup tickets on an average of 25,000 tickets per month were distributed, representing a sum of £4986-12-4. Cost of printing £13-7-8.

Alfons. Maria Galea
Hon. Treasurer
20 January 1919

---

7   *Ibid.* 3 November 1919

BIBLIOGRAPHY AND REFERENCES

Newspapers

Local
Times of Malta
The Sunday Times (Malta)
Daily Malta Chronicle
Malta Independent on Sunday

Foreign
The Daily Mail (U.K.)

Texts

Call-Out, A wartime diary of air/sea rescue operations at Malta, Frederick R. Galea, 2002.

Malta: An Aviation History by Alfred Coldman, 2001.

Submarines and Targets: Suggestions for New Codified Rules of Submarine Warfare, Georgetown

Rules of Submarine Warfare, Georgetown Law Journal, Jane Gilliland, 1985

Military Aviation in Malta G.C. 1915–1993, A Comprehensive History, John F. Hamlin, 1994.

Gallipoli: The Malta Connection, by John Anthony Mizzi, 1991.

HM Dockyard, Malta, W.A Griffiths, 1917.

The Maltese Public Service 1800–1940: The Administrative Politics of a Micro-State, Godfrey A. Pirotta, 1996.

Malta's Grand Harbour and its Environs in War and Peace, Dr Charles J. Boffa, 2000.

L-Istorja tat-Tarzna, Karmenu Ellul Galea, 1973.

The Knights of St John in the British Empire, by Colonel E.J. King, St John's Gate London, 1934.

Military Hospitals in Malta, C. Savona-Ventura.

Royal Navy Hospital, Malta, the sick quarters of his Royal Highness Prince Alfred, The Illustrated London News, April, 1863.

Military Hospitals in Malta, C. Savona-Ventura.

British Malta, A.V. Laferla, Vol II.

Britain in the Mediterranean & the defence of her naval stations, Quentin Hughes, 1981.

The British Fortifications, An Illustrated Guide to the British Fortifications in Malta, Stephen C. Spiteri, 1991.

Education in Malta, J. Zammit Mangion, 1992.

The Naval War in the Mediterranean, 1914–1918, Paul G. Halpern, 1987.

Military Hospitals in Malta during the War, G.R. Bruce, MA, MD, Capt. RAMC.

History of the Royal Malta Artillery, Abridged for use in Regimental Schools; Criterion Press, Valletta 1944.

R.A.M.C Training 1935, H.M.S.O, 1935.

San Giljan mitt sena parrocca 1891–1991 – The Centenary of a parish, St Julian's; Deer Publications, Edited by Stanley Fiorini, 1992.

X'kien gara sew fis-Sette Giugno, Paul Bartolo, 1979.

Il-Gwerra tad-Dinja (1914–1918), Duminku Degiorgio.

L-Istorja ta' L-Avjazzjoni f'Malta, Richard J. Caruana, 2002; Pubblikazzjonijiet Indipendenza.

Reference Books

Maltese Biographies of the Twentieth Century, 1997, Edition, by Michael J. Schiavone and Louis J. Scerri,

The Penguin Hansard, Volume III, Britain Gathers Strength, Taken verbatim from the House of Commons Official Report of Parliamentary Debates, Penguin Books, August 1941

Il-Gbira Guerra tad-Dinja, Vol. I-IV, Opra Colossali li tigbor fiha l-ahjar fattijet tal guerra mehuda minn fuk cotba ta potenzi nuetrali Propieta' Letteraria u Artistica ta Andolfo & Magro, Stamperija u Legatorija ta' Emilio Lombardi, 28, Strada Santa Maria, u 27, 28, Strada San Trofimo Sliema (1922).

Melita Historica

The Collins History of the World in the Twentieth Century, J.A.S Grenville, 1994.

Report on the Elementary Schools' Department for 1915–1916, Elementary Schools' Office, Malta, 20 April, 1916

Reports and Plans of the Capuccini Naval Cemetery, Rinella, Malta

Purnell's History of the Second World War, 1973

Journals/Magazines/Maps

Malta at War, 1978 by Richard Muscat; Progress Press Co. Ltd.

Lehen il-Banda Cittadina "Sliema", Festa tal-Madonna tas-Sacro Cuor, 2002

La Diocesi, Malta

Hitler's Third, 2001

Journal for Historical Review, feature, A Son's Struggle for His Father's Honor, The Life and Death of My Father, Rudolf Hess, 1992.

Towards Responsible Government, Historical Background of Constitutional Developments up to 1921, by Dr R. Farrugia Randon M.D. FR. Hist. S. (Lond) which appeared in the Report and Accounts of the Mid-Med Group of 1993.

Provvedimenti presi dal Governo per il sollievo per il sollievo delle classi lavoratrici e povere di queste Isole, Malta Stamperia di Governo, 1919

Journal of the American Medical Association of 28 December, 1918

JB Stamp Auctions.

Yearbook of the Medial Missionaries of Mary, Healing & Development, 2002 Edition

Imperial War Museum, Information Sheet No. 38: The Women's Royal Naval Service in the First World War, 2001

Department of Information, Speech delivered by the Acting President of Malta, Dr George Hyzler during the Annual European Congress of Regional Anesthesia held at the Mediterranean Conference Centre, Valletta on 10 September 2003.

National Tourist Organisation, 1996. The Military Heritage of the Maltese Islands (Map).

Websites

www.naval-history.net
http://www.harboro.ndirect.co.uk/malta.htm
http://louishenwood.com/history/no29.html
www.sja-haltonhills.org
http:website.lineone.net/-remosliema/chambray.htm
http://www.armeniangenocideposters.org/html/foreign
www.plaques.satlink.com.au

Acknowledgements

I am indebted to many people who have given me their undivided attention. My gratitude goes to all without whose assistance, it would have been impossible to complete this research. My apologies if, I might have left someone out:

- **My wife, Petronela and my mother, Mary.**
- **Family Zammit-Dimech** who supplied me with information related to John Ellul who died on HMS *Louvain* and also for encouraging me to write on the Great War.
- **Mr Andrew Cauchi of Gudja**, merits quite an introduction as he has been the mainstay of my research for his keen interest in indicating useful sources and providing me with a wealth of material, re: Maltese casualties suffered during the First World War, prisoner of war camps, photos, and other interesting data for the book. Many thanks also go to him for writing the foreword.

Mr Cauchi has followed in his father's footsteps in the art of collection and appreciation of militaria, memorabilia and ephemera as well as numismatics and was certainly a very useful source, especially in the area of Melitensia, in the course of my research.

His father Giuseppe Cauchi (1922–2000) was a keen numismatic and militaria collector. In the near future, Andrew intends to publish research that he is presently undertaking. Mr Cauchi has contributed in the writing of features in Band Club Programmes and also participated in several television and radio programmes on the subject of numistmatics and militaria.

- **Ms Lina Brockdorff M.A. of Ibraġġ** for assisting me in the proof-reading.
- **Mr Charles Mizzi, (Permanent Secretary, Ministry of Education)** for his interest in my work and also for useful hints on pre-Great War history.
- **Mr Charles Stafrace (Director Corporate Services and Policy Implementation)** in the Ministry of Education for indicating valuable sources of Aviation History.
- **Mr Charles Cilia (Assistant Director)** in the Teachers' Documentation and Resources Centre and his staff, Education Department at Floriana for their assistance in indicating Education Department Circulars, Notes, Communications and Memos for the period 1914–1919.
- **The Staff of Beltissebħ library**.
- **The Management and Staff of the Tourist Information Office** that falls under the auspices of the Malta Tourism Authority and the Ministry of Tourism for taking time to find the right source of information for my research.
- **Louis Henwood of Senglea**, for allowing to use the story of the *Polverista* explosion of the Malta Dockyard in the First World War when his wife's grandfather lost his life.
- **Charles Bezzina of Gozo**, (son of the late Frank Bezzina), poet, historian and researcher about Gozitan history. Mr Bezzina provided me with the list of Gozitan casualties and background history about the casualties, which

he painstakingly researched and kindly allowed me to reproduce and translate into English for presentation in my book.

- **Mr Raymond Cachia of Mqabba** for providing information about his grandfather who served during the Great War and also for allowing me to view postcards sent by his grandfather during service overseas.
- **Mr Winston Zammit, B.A Hons, M.A, of Sliema** for providing me with unpublished and published research, which he undertook, and kindly allowing me to add it to my work. He also provided me with several articles from magazines on areas related to my research.
- **Miss Christine Scicluna of Sliema**, for lending me texts, magazines and photos.
- **Alfred Fenech of Attard**, for helping me with his vast collection of interesting objects and written material.
- **Mr Stephen Petroni** of the Arms, Armour and Militaria Society (AAMS).